Become a top fact-fetcher with CGP!

Quick question — do you own CGP's
Knowledge Organiser for Edexcel GCSE Chemistry?

You do? Great! Now you can use this Knowledge Retriever
to check you've really remembered all the crucial facts.

There are two memory tests for each topic, plus mixed quiz questions
to make extra sure it's all stuck in your brain. Enjoy.

CGP — still the best! ☺

Our sole aim here at CGP is to produce the highest quality books —
carefully written, immaculately presented and dangerously close to being funny.

Then we work our socks off to get them out to you
— at the cheapest possible prices.

Contents

Topic 6 — Groups in the Periodic Table

Topic 7 — Rates of Reaction and Energy Changes

Topic 8 — Fuels and Earth Science

Topic 9 — Separate Chemistry 2

Core Practicals

Practical Skills

Published by CGP.
From original material by Richard Parsons.

Editors: Emma Clayton, Emily Forsberg, Sarah Pattison and George Wright.
Contributor: Paddy Gannon.

With thanks to Sharon Keeley-Holden for the proofreading.
With thanks to Emily Smith for the copyright research.

ISBN: 978 1 78908 853 3

Hazard symbols used on p.15-16 contain public sector information published by the Health and Safety Executive and licensed under the Open Government Licence. http://www.nationalarchives.gov.uk/doc/open-government-licence/version/3/

Printed by Elanders Ltd, Newcastle upon Tyne.
Clipart from Corel®
Illustrations by: Sandy Gardner Artist, email sandy@sandygardner.co.uk

How to Use This Book

Every page in this book has a matching page in the GCSE Chemistry **Knowledge Organiser**. Before using this book, try to **memorise** everything on a Knowledge Organiser page. Then follow these **seven steps** to see how much knowledge you're able to retrieve...

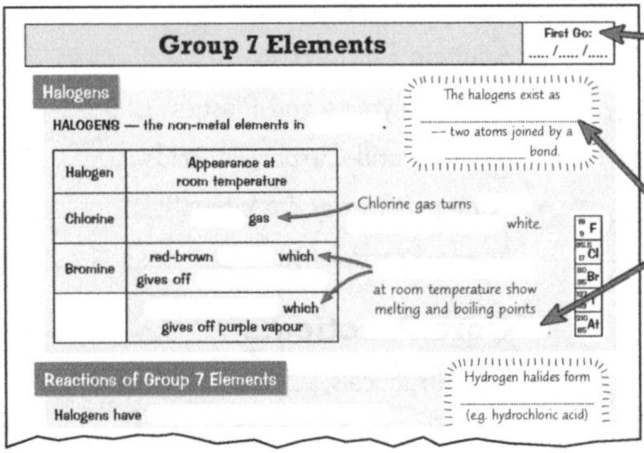

1. In this book, there are two versions of each page. Find the **'First Go'** of the page you've tried to memorise, and write the **date** at the top.

2. Use what you've learned from the Knowledge Organiser to **fill in** any dotted lines or white spaces.

   You may need to draw, complete or add labels to diagrams too.

3. Use the Knowledge Organiser to **check your work**. Use a **different colour pen** to write in anything you missed or that wasn't quite right. This lets you see clearly what you **know** and what you **don't know**.

4. After doing the First Go page, **wait a few days**. This is important because **spacing out** your retrieval practice helps you to remember things better.

5. Now do the **Second Go** page.

   The Second Go page is harder — it has more things missing.

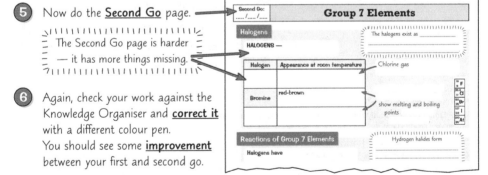

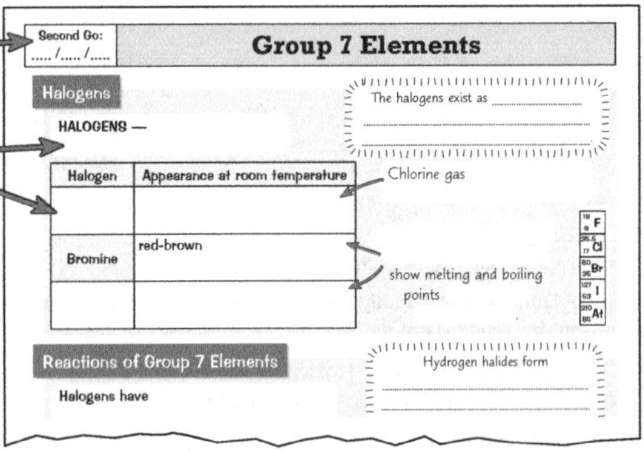

6. Again, check your work against the Knowledge Organiser and **correct it** with a different colour pen. You should see some **improvement** between your first and second go.

7. **Wait** another few days, then try recreating the whole Knowledge Organiser page on a **blank piece of paper**. If you can do this, you'll know you've **really learned it**.

There are also **Mixed Practice Quizzes** dotted throughout the book:

- The quizzes come in sets of four. They test a mix of content from the previous few pages.
- Do each quiz on a different day — write the date you do each one at the top of the quiz.
- Tick the questions you get right and record your score in the box at the end.

The Scientific Method

First Go:
..... / /

Developing Theories

Come up with [_____]

↓

[_____]

↓

Evidence is peer-reviewed

↓

If all evidence backs up [_____], it becomes an [_____].

HYPOTHESIS — a possible [_____] for [_____].

PEER REVIEW — when other scientists check results and explanations before [_____].

[_____] can still change over time [_____], e.g. the theory of atomic structure:

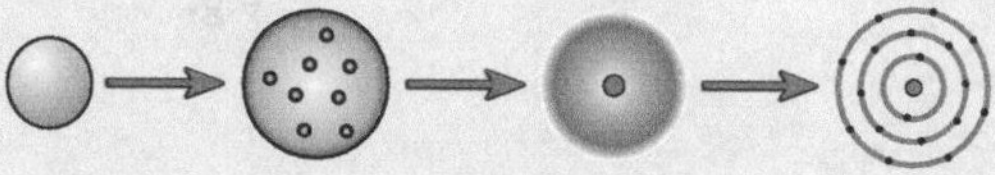

Models

REPRESENTATIONAL MODELS — a simplified [_____] of the [_____], e.g. the different ways of showing covalent bonding:

[_____]

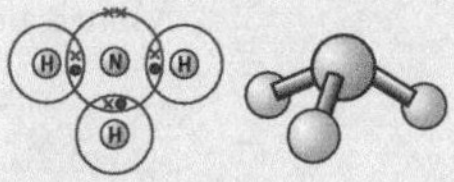

Models help scientists explain and make

COMPUTATIONAL MODELS — computers are used to [_____] complex processes.

Issues in Science

[_____] can create four types of issue:

① Economic — e.g. beneficial [_____], like alternative energy sources, may be too [____] to use.

② Environmental — e.g. [_____] could [____] the natural environment.

③ Social — [_____] based on research can affect people, e.g. [_____] fossil fuels.

④ Personal — some decisions affect [_____], e.g. a person may not want a wind farm being built [_____].

Media reports on scientific developments may be, inaccurate or

Hazard and Risk

HAZARD — something that could [_____].

RISK — the [_____] that a [_____] will cause harm.

Hazards associated with chemistry experiments include:

....
e.g. sulfuric acid

Faulty equipment

.... from Bunsen burners

The seriousness of the and the likelihood of both need consideration.

 ☑ ☑ ☑

Second Go: ...../...../.....

The Scientific Method

Developing Theories

Come up with

↓

↓

Evidence is

↓

If

HYPOTHESIS —

PEER REVIEW —

can still change over time ,
e.g. :

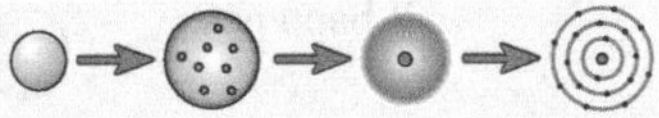

Models

REPRESENTATIONAL MODELS — a , e.g. the different ways of :

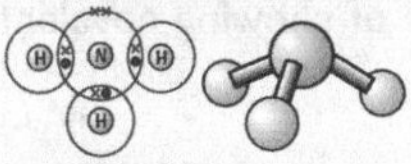

COMPUTATIONAL MODELS —

Models help scientists explain ....

Issues in Science

....
can create four types of issue:

1. Economic —
2.
3. Social —
4. Personal —

.... on scientific developments may be ....

Hazard and Risk

HAZARD —

RISK —

.... associated with chemistry experiments include:

The .... both need consideration.

Designing & Performing Experiments

First Go: ..... /..... /.....

Collecting Data

Data should be...

REPEATABLE	Same person gets after repeating experiment using the and equipment.
	Similar results can be achieved by , or by using a different method or piece of .
ACCURATE	Results are to the .
	All data is close to .

Reliable data is .... and ....

Valid results are .... and .... and answer the ....

Fair Tests

INDEPENDENT VARIABLE	Variable that you .
VARIABLE	Variable that is .
VARIABLE	Variable that is .
	An experiment kept under as without anything being done to it.
	An experiment where only the changes, whilst all other variables are kept .

.... are carried out when .... can't be controlled.

Four Things to Look Out For

1. RANDOM ERRORS — differences caused by things like in measuring.
2. SYSTEMATIC ERRORS — measurements that are wrong by each time.
3. ZERO ERRORS — systematic errors that are caused by using that isn't .
4. ANOMALOUS RESULTS — results that with the rest of the data.

Anomalous results can be .... if you know ....

Processing Data

Calculate the — add together measurements and number of measurements.

UNCERTAINTY — the amount by which a may differ from the .

uncertainty =

measurement minus

In any calculation, you should round the answer to the .... number of significant figures (s.f.) given.

Second Go: ..... /..... /.....

Designing & Performing Experiments

Collecting Data

Data should be...

	Same person gets
	Similar results can be

Reliable data

Valid results

.... can't be controlled.

Fair Tests

INDEPENDENT VARIABLE —
— an experiment kept under
— an experiment where

Four Things to Look Out For

1. RANDOM ERRORS —
2. SYSTEMATIC ERRORS —
3. ZERO ERRORS —
4. ANOMALOUS RESULTS —

Anomalous results ....

Processing Data

— add together all measurements and divide by .

UNCERTAINTY —

uncertainty =

In any calculation, ...

Presenting Data

First Go: ..... / ..... / .....

Bar Charts

Bar charts can be used when independent variable is ____ or ____.

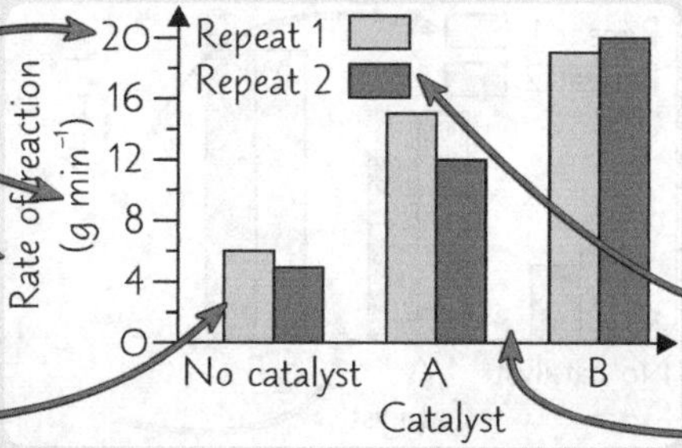

____ → 20

units

____ axes

bars same ____

Discrete data can only take .... with no ....

Key — used when there are ____.

____ between categories

Plotting Graphs

Graphs can be used when ____ variables are ____.

.... data — can take .... within a range.

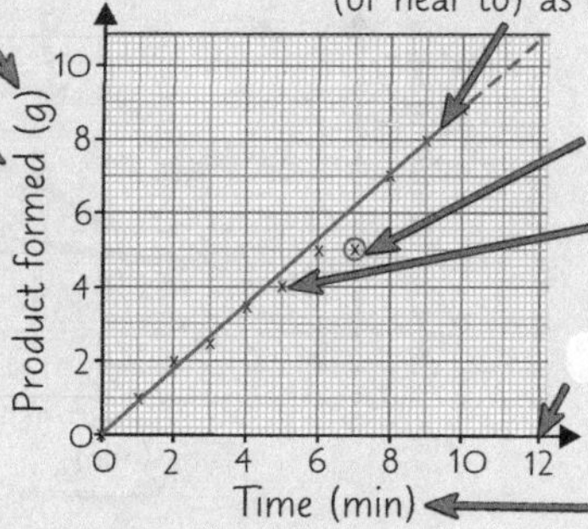

____ variable on y-axis

units

____ through (or near to) as many points as possible

Gradient tells you how quickly ____ ____ changes if you change the ____.

____

points marked with ____ cross

____ scale on axes

gradient = ____

____

____ variable on x-axis

Three Types of Correlation Between Variables

1 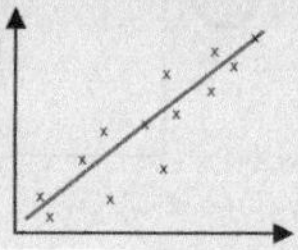

____ correlation

2 

Inverse (____) correlation

3 

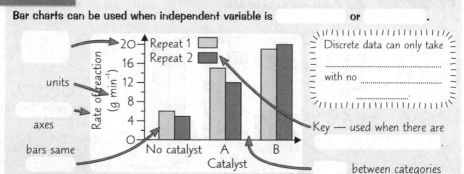

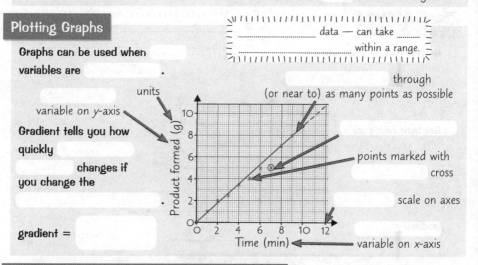

____

Possible reasons for a correlation:

Chance — correlation might be ____.

Third variable — ____ the two variables.

Cause — if every other variable that ____ the result is controlled, you can conclude that changing one variable ____ in the other.

☐ ☐ ☐

Second Go:
...../...../.....

Presenting Data

Bar Charts

Bar charts can be used when

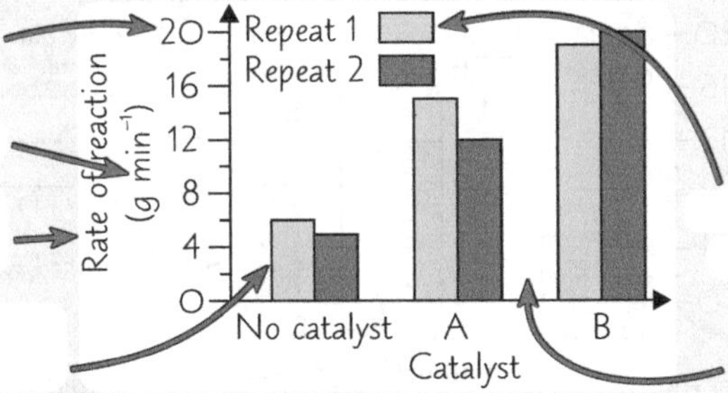

— used when there are

.

Plotting Graphs

Graphs can be used when

— can take

.

(or near to)

Gradient tells you

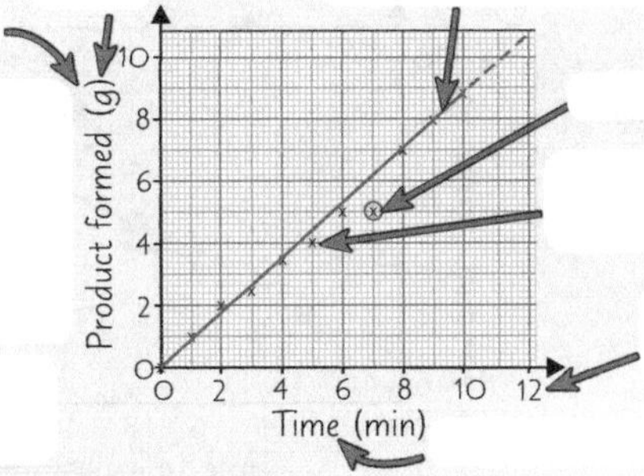

gradient =

variable on

Three Types of Correlation Between Variables

1

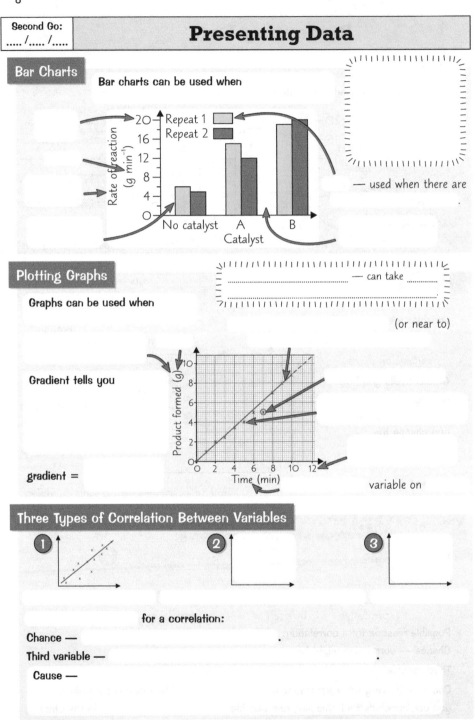

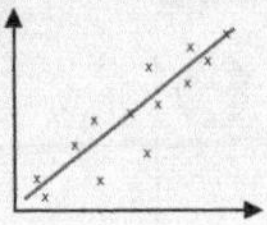

2

3

for a correlation:

Chance — .

Third variable — .

Cause —

Conclusions, Evaluations and Units

First Go: ..... /..... /.....

Conclusions

Draw conclusion by stating ____ between ____ variables.

↓

Justify conclusion using ____.

↓

Refer to ____ and state whether ____.

You can only draw a conclusion from .... — you can't go any further than that.

Evaluations

EVALUATION — a ____ of the whole investigation.

	Things to consider
____	• Validity of ____ • ____ variables
Results	• ____, accuracy, ____ and ____ of results • Number of ____ taken • Level of ____ in the results
____ results	• Causes of any ____ results

You could make more predictions based on ...., which you could test ....

Repeating experiment with changes to improve the ____ will give you more ____ in your conclusions.

S.I. Units

S.I. BASE UNITS — a set of ____ that ____ use.

Quantity	S.I. Unit
____	kilogram (____)
length	____
____	second (____)
____ of a substance	____

Scaling Units

SCALING PREFIX — a word or ____ that goes ____ a unit to indicate a ____.

Multiple of unit	Prefix
10^{12}	
10^{9}	
	____ (M)
	kilo (____)
0.1	deci (d)
	centi (____)
0.001	
	micro (____)
10^{-9}	

kg ⇄ g (____ / ____)

____

÷1000 ⇅ ×1000

dm^3

÷1000 ⇅ ×1000

____

Second Go:
..... /..... /.....

Conclusions, Evaluations and Units

Conclusions

Draw conclusion by between

.

Justify conclusion .

Refer to .

You can only draw a conclusion ....
....
.... — you can't
....
....

Evaluations

EVALUATION —

	Things to consider
	• •
	• • •
	•

You could ....
....
based on your conclusion,
....
....
....

Repeating experiment

S.I. Units

S.I. BASE UNITS —

....
....
....

Quantity	S.I. Unit
	kilogram (kg)
length	

Scaling Units

SCALING PREFIX —

Multiple of unit	Prefix
	deci (d)
	centi (c)

Mixed Practice Quizzes

It's time for some quick quizzes to test you on p.3-10. Understanding how science works is super important, so give these quizzes a go and see how you get on.

Quiz 1

Date: ...... / ...... / ......

1) Give the equation used to find the gradient of a straight line on a graph.
2) When can an anomalous result in a data set be ignored?
3) Give two ways in which models can be useful to scientists.
4) Which term is given to a possible explanation for an observation?
5) What is an 'evaluation' of an investigation?
6) Give two examples of S.I. base units, and the quantities they are used to measure.
7) What two things must be considered when assessing a hazard?
8) When is it necessary to include a key in a bar chart?
9) How can you calculate the uncertainty of a mean value?
10) When might you need to carry out a control experiment?

Total:

Quiz 2

Date: ...... / ...... / ......

1) What is the range of a set of data?
2) Describe how to calculate the mean of a set of values.
3) When would you use a bar chart to represent data?
4) What can cause an accepted theory or model to change over time?
5) State the S.I. base unit for mass.
6) True or false? A conclusion cannot go beyond what the data shows.
7) What is a dependent variable?
8) Which type of model shows a real system as a simplified picture?
9) What is an anomalous result?
10) Give two types of issue that can result from scientific developments.

Total:

Mixed Practice Quizzes

Quiz 3

Date: ...... / ...... / ......

1) Give a hazard that is associated with chemistry experiments.
2) What makes an experiment a fair test?
3) What is meant by the term 'S.I. base unit'?
4) Give one issue associated with media reports on scientific developments.
5) What is meant by the term 'reliable data'?
6) What is peer review?
7) Give two reasons why a correlation between two variables does not always mean that changing one causes the change in the other.
8) True or false? The independent variable is shown on a graph's y-axis.
9) Give an example of an impact of a scientific development on individuals.
10) What is meant by the term 'uncertainty' when describing data?

Total:

Quiz 4

Date: ...... / ...... / ......

1) Give a suitable way to display data where both variables are continuous.
2) Give four examples of things to consider when evaluating an investigation.
3) True or false? A risk is something that could potentially cause harm.
4) What are random errors in an experiment?
5) Which scaling prefix indicates a multiplying factor of 0.001?
6) Give an example of an accepted theory that has changed over time.
7) Define the term 'systematic error'.
8) What is a control variable?
9) Define each of the following terms:
   a) Accurate data
   b) Precise data
   c) Valid results
10) How should a straight line of best fit be drawn on a graph?

Total:

Chemical Equations

First Go: ..... /..... /.....

Chemical Formulas and Equations

CHEMICAL FORMULA — shows the in a compound.

E.g. CO_2 ← for every carbon atom

CHEMICAL EQUATION — shows the in a reaction.

	....			Products		
.... :	methane	+	oxygen →	....	+	water
Symbol equation:	....	+	$2O_2$ →	CO_2	+	....

Symbol equations must have on each side so the equation is .

Balance equations by writing in front of the to add more units of that .

State Symbols

(s)	
(l)	
	gas
	aqueous

Common Chemical Formulas

Name	Formula
	H_2O
	NH_3
Carbon dioxide	
	H_2
Chlorine	
Oxygen	

Name	Formula
Ammonium	
Hydroxide	
Nitrate	NO_3^-
	CO_3^{2-}
	SO_4^{2-}

Ionic Equations

IONIC EQUATIONS — show only that react and .

Ionic equations don't include .... ions that are ....

 calcium chloride + aqueous sodium → calcium hydroxide +

$_{(aq)}$ + $2OH^-_{(aq)}$ →

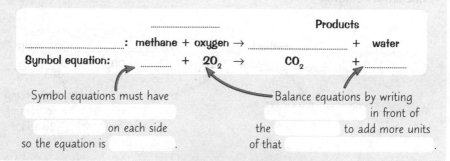

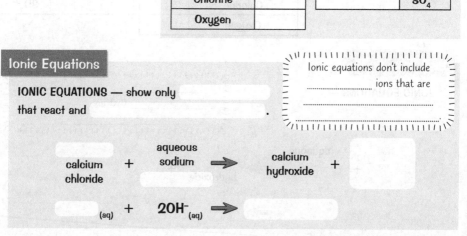

Second Go: ...../...../.....

Chemical Equations

Chemical Formulas and Equations

CHEMICAL FORMULA —

E.g. CO_2 ⟵

CHEMICAL EQUATION — .

....

..........................: **methane +** .... → .... **+ water**

..........................: .... **+** $2O_2$ → CO_2 **+** ....

Symbol equations must have

equations by writing in front of

the to add

.

State Symbols

(s)	

Common Chemical Formulas

Name	Formula
	H_2
Chlorine	
Oxygen	

Name	Formula
	NO_3^-
	CO_3^{2-}
	SO_4^{2-}

Ionic Equations

IONIC EQUATIONS —

.... don't include .... that are ....

....

+ **aqueous** → **hydroxide** +

→

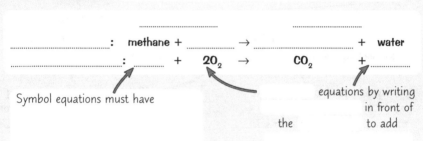

Hazards and History of the Atom

First Go: ..... /..... /.....

Hazard Symbols

Understanding .... means you can use .... when working with the substances.

HAZARD SYMBOLS — warn you about ....

Oxidising

....

....

Highly ....

.... Harmful

.... hazard

When planning an experiment, ... — identify .... and their risks, and suggest ....

The History of the Atom

Start of 1800s ← John Dalton described atoms as ....

.... — ball of .... containing .... electrons. → 1897

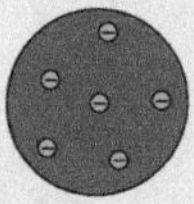

Nuclear model — .... surrounded by a cloud of .... (and mostly ....). → 1909

.... are fired at thin sheet...

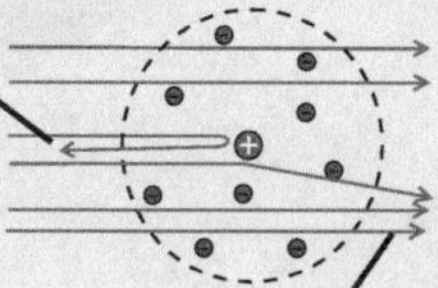

...some are deflected backwards...

... . pass straight through.

.... — electrons orbit nucleus .... → 1913

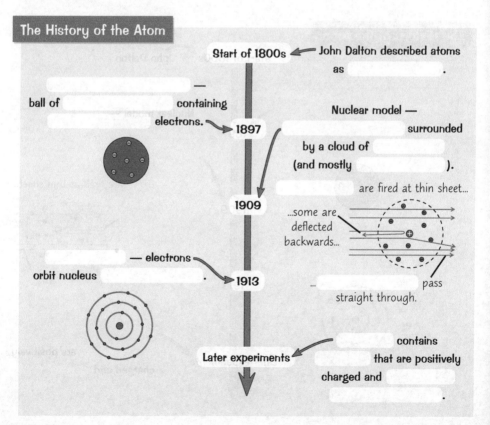

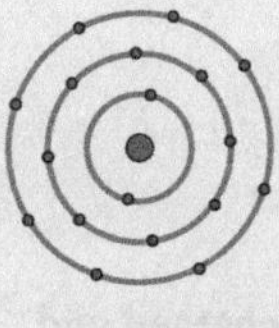

Later experiments ← .... contains .... that are positively charged and ....

Second Go: ..... /..... /.....

Hazards and History of the Atom

Hazard Symbols

HAZARD SYMBOLS —

....
means you can use ....
....
....

When planning an experiment,

The History of the Atom

Start of 1800s — John Dalton

1897

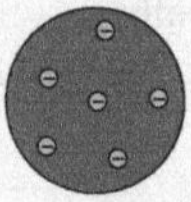

Nuclear model —

1909

are fired at thin sheet...

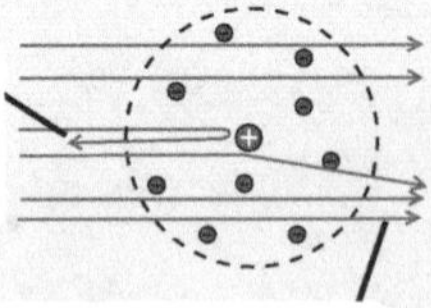

1913

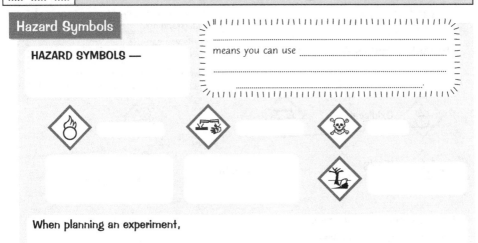

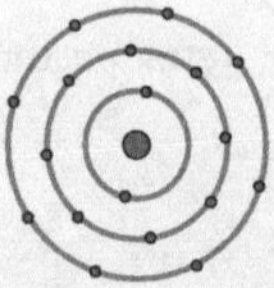

Later experiments

are positively charged and .

Atoms, Elements and Isotopes

First Go: ..... / ..... / .....

Atomic Structure

Radius of ______ ______ 10^{-10} m.

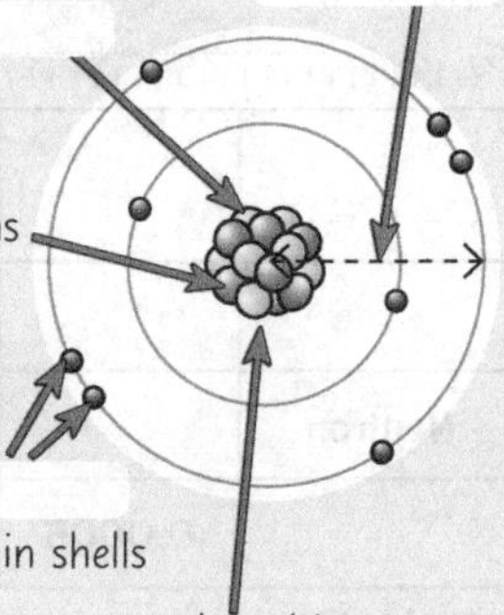

protons

______ orbiting in shells

nucleus (tiny compared to ______)

Atoms have no overall charge because ....

Particle	Relative mass	Relative charge
Proton		+1
Neutron	1	
	0.0005	–1

Most of .... of an atom is in ....

Nuclear Symbols

NUCLEAR SYMBOL — used to describe atoms:

______ = total number of protons and neutrons in an atom

______

$^{23}_{11}\text{Na}$

number of .... = ... number – .... number

atomic number = number ______

Elements

ELEMENTS — substances made up of atoms with ______ ______.

Different elements have different ...., so each element has a ....

______ of an element — atoms with ______ number of protons but ______ of neutrons.

Relative Atomic Mass

RELATIVE ATOMIC MASS (A_r) — ______ of one atom of an element, compared to ______ ______ of one atom of carbon-12:

$$A_r = \frac{\text{sum of (\_\_\_\_\_\_ × isotope mass number)}}{\text{total \_\_\_\_\_\_ of all isotopes}}$$

A_r might not be a whole number because it's .... taking into account ....

Second Go: ...../...../.....

Atoms, Elements and Isotopes

Atomic Structure

Radius

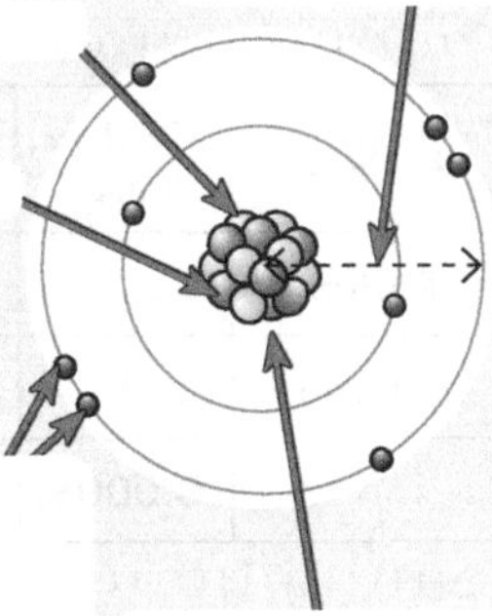

Atoms have no .... because ....

		+1
Neutron		
	0.0005	

Nuclear Symbols

NUCLEAR SYMBOL

— used to :

= total number of

$^{23}_{11}\text{Na}$

number of ....
= ....
....

Elements

ELEMENTS —

Different elements ...., so each element ....

Relative Atomic Mass

RELATIVE ATOMIC MASS (A_r) —

, compared to

:

$$A_r = \frac{\text{sum of } (\qquad\qquad)}{\text{total}}$$

.... might not be a whole number because ....

The Periodic Table

First Go: ..... /..... /.....

Mendeleev's Table

Mendeleev made his Table of Elements by ______ using their ______.

If he ordered the elements by ______, he could arrange them so ______ ______ formed columns.

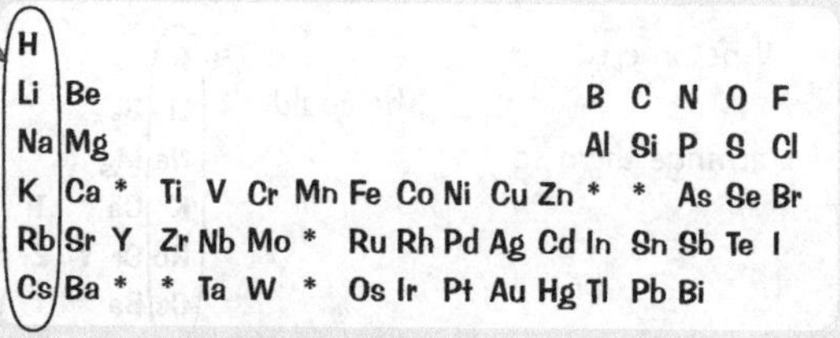

H
Li Be B C N O F
Na Mg Al Si P S Cl
K Ca * Ti V Cr Mn Fe Co Ni Cu Zn * * As Se Br
Rb Sr Y Zr Nb Mo * Ru Rh Pd Ag Cd In Sn Sb Te I
Cs Ba * * Ta W * Os Ir Pt Au Hg Tl Pb Bi

Mendeleev ______ ______ in places where ordering by ______ didn't fit the pattern.

Some of the ______ he used were wrong due to ______.

Mendeleev left gaps in the table to ______ ______.

He ______ of missing elements using the ______ in the columns.

The Modern Periodic Table

The ______ are ordered by ______.

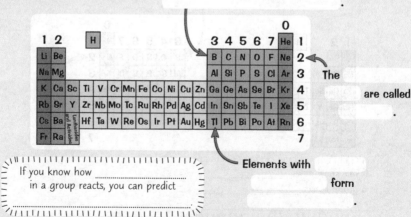

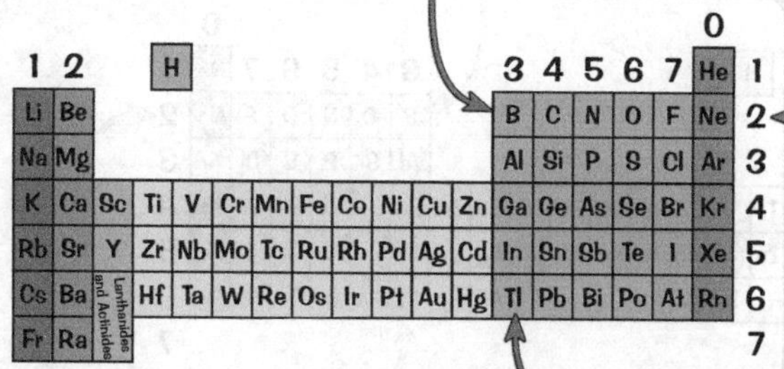

The ______ ______ are called ______.

Elements with ______ ______ form ______.

If you know how .... in a group reacts, you can predict ....

______ tells you the electronic configuration:

Group number = the number of electrons in the ______.

______ = the number of shells with electrons in.

Second Go: ..... /..... /.....

The Periodic Table

Mendeleev's Table

Mendeleev made his Table of Elements

If he ordered , he could arrange them so .

H																
Li	Be											B	C	N	O	F
Na	Mg											Al	Si	P	S	Cl
K	Ca	*	Ti	V	Cr	Mn	Fe	Co	Ni	Cu	Zn	*	*	As	Se	Br
Rb	Sr	Y	Zr	Nb	Mo	*	Ru	Rh	Pd	Ag	Cd	In	Sn	Sb	Te	I
Cs	Ba	*	*	Ta	W	*	Os	Ir	Pt	Au	Hg	Tl	Pb	Bi		

Mendeleev

in places where .

Some of the

Mendeleev left gaps

He

of missing elements using .

The Modern Periodic Table

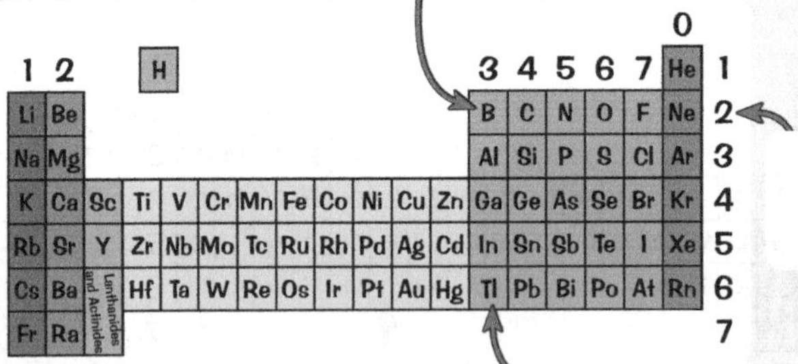

If you know how ....
in a group reacts, ...
....

tells you the :

Group number = .

= the number of .

Mixed Practice Quizzes

Here are some quick-fire quiz questions to test what you've done on p.13-20. No — don't mention it. Mark each test yourself and tot up your score.

Quiz 1

Date: ...... / ...... / ......

1) How does the size of a nucleus compare to the overall size of an atom?
2) What is the overall charge of an atom?
3) How did Mendeleev group elements in his Table of Elements?
4) True or false? Isotopes of an element have different numbers of neutrons.
5) Which part of an atom's nuclear symbol shows the number of protons it contains?
6) What does the chemical formula of a compound show?
7) What was Dalton's model of the atom?
8) What is the chemical formula for a hydrogen molecule?
9) Why is the information provided by hazard symbols useful?
10) What is relative atomic mass (A_r)?

Total:

Quiz 2

Date: ...... / ...... / ......

1) True or false? The nucleus of an atom is negatively charged.
2) What does an ionic equation show?
3) What does the atomic number tell you about an atom?
4) How is the relative atomic mass (A_r) of an element calculated?
5) Why were some of the atomic masses Mendeleev used to make his Table of Elements wrong?
6) What is the relative charge of an electron?
7) What name is given to the horizontal rows of the periodic table?
8) Which state of matter is indicated by the symbol (s)?
9) What does an element's group number tell you about its electronic configuration?
10) What did Mendeleev use to predict the properties of elements missing from his Table of Elements?

Total:

Mixed Practice Quizzes

Quiz 3

Date: ...... / ...... / ......

1) Where is the mass of an atom concentrated?
2) True or false? Each of the particles that make up an atom have the same relative mass.
3) In chemical equations, why are large numbers used in front of chemical formulas?
4) What is the state symbol for a liquid?
5) What is the relative mass of a neutron?
6) What does the mass number tell you about an atom?
7) Describe the 'plum pudding' model of the atom.
8) What does an element's period number tell you about its electronic configuration?
9) True or false? The atomic number of an atom is equal to the number of neutrons in that atom.
10) What does the hazard symbol '!' mean?

Total:

Quiz 4

Date: ...... / ...... / ......

1) What name is given to the positively-charged particles in an atom?
2) How does the mass of an electron compare to the mass of a proton?
3) What are isotopes of an element?
4) Give the chemical formula for each of the following compounds and ions:
   a) water b) ammonia c) nitrate ion d) carbonate ion
5) Give two types of chemical equation.
6) How many oxygen atoms are present in one molecule of CO_2?
7) Which atomic model shows electrons orbiting the nucleus in fixed shells?
8) What does the state symbol (aq) tell you about a substance?
9) How are the elements ordered in the modern periodic table?
10) What should you think about when doing a risk assessment?

Total:

Electronic Configurations and Ions

First Go: ..... /..... /.....

Electronic Configurations

Electrons occupy — sometimes called energy .

Electrons before occupying a new one, starting with the .

Shell	allowed in shell
1	2
2	
	8

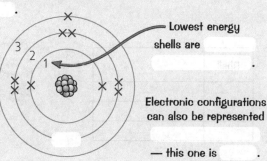

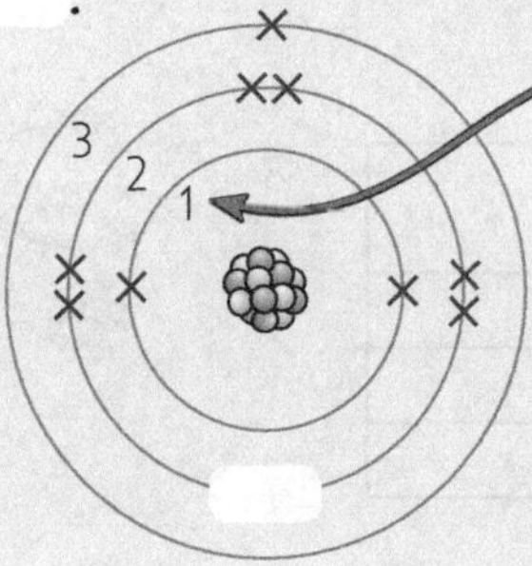

Lowest energy shells are .

Electronic configurations can also be represented — this one is .

Forming Ions

IONS — made when are transferred.

	Electron transfer	Group	Charge of ion
Metals	electrons to form ions (cations)		
		2	
Non-metals	electrons to form ions ( )	6	
			1–

Charge on ion = gained or lost.

E.g. means 2 electrons (so there are 2 more).

The .... formed by elements in these groups have ....

Ionic Formulas

The of any ionic compound is .

Calcium = $Ca(NO_3)_2$ (2+, 1–)

Overall charge is as there are for each .

Name ends in...	Anion contains...
-ate	...
	...only one element.

Except for , OH^-.

Second Go: ..... /..... /.....

Electronic Configurations and Ions

Electronic Configurations

Electrons occupy .

Electrons

Shell	

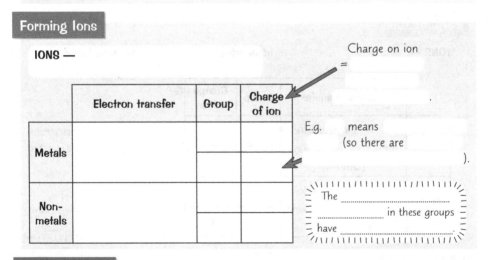

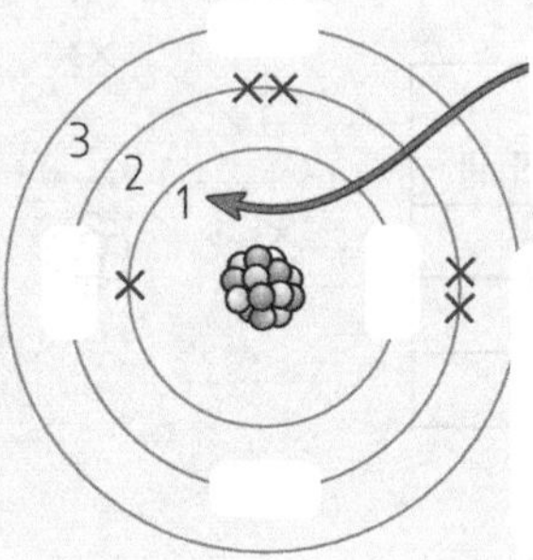

Electronic configurations

Forming Ions

IONS —

Charge on ion =

	Electron transfer	Group	Charge of ion
Metals			
Non-metals			

.

E.g. means (so there are).

The .... in these groups have ....

Ionic Formulas

....

....

= $Ca(NO_3)_2$

Overall charge

Name ends in...	Anion contains...
	...
	...

Except for ....

Ionic Substances & Bonding Models

First Go: ..... /..... /.....

Ionic Bonding

IONIC BONDING — ______
between ______.
Ionic bonds form when ______ are transferred
from metal atoms to ______.

Sodium Chloride

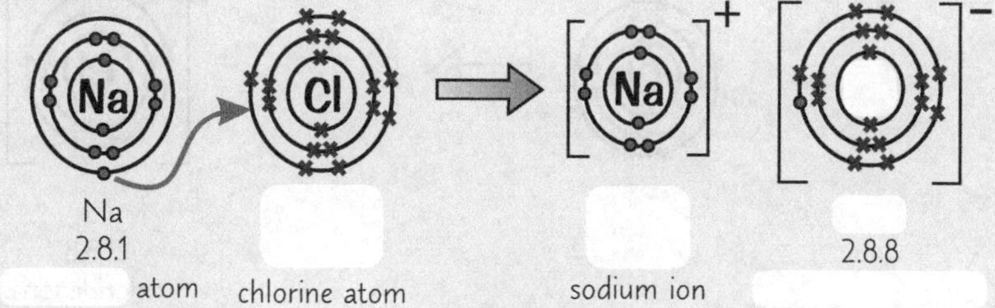

Giant Ionic Lattice

______
______ of attraction between oppositely charged ions act ______.

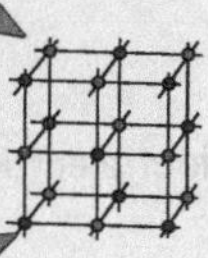

______
regular arrangement of ______.

Three Properties of Ionic Compounds

1. High ______ points — lots of energy needed to ______ ______ ______.
2. ______ in water.
3. Conduct electricity only when ______ ______ — ions free to move and ______.

Models

Ball and stick diagrams:

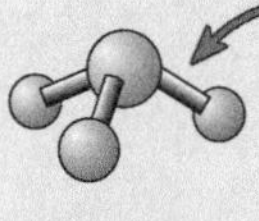

doesn't show ______ the electrons in the ______ come from.

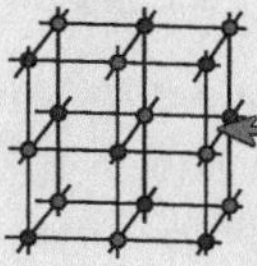

not ______, has ______ between ions.

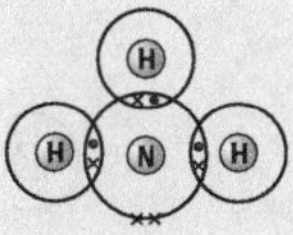

Dot and cross diagrams — don't show ______ ______ or their ______ in space.

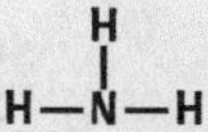

Displayed formula (2D) — doesn't show ______ ______.

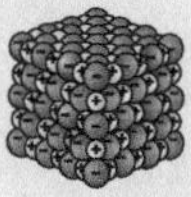

______ — only shows outer layer.

Second Go:
...../...../.....

Ionic Substances & Bonding Models

Ionic Bonding

IONIC BONDING — ....

.... Ionic bonds form when ....

....

Sodium Chloride

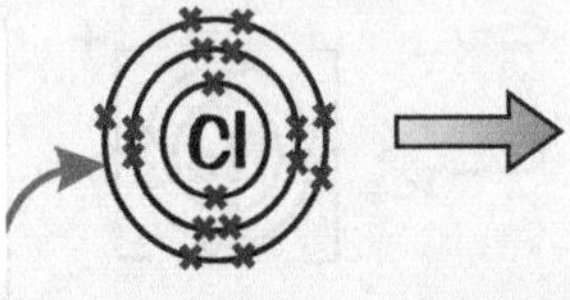

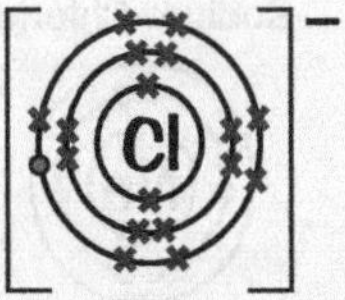

Cl^-
2.8.8
chloride ion

Giant Ionic Lattice

of attraction between

.

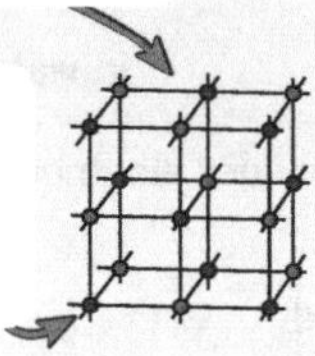

Three Properties of Ionic Compounds

1.

2.

3. **Conduct electricity only when**

Models

Ball and stick diagrams:

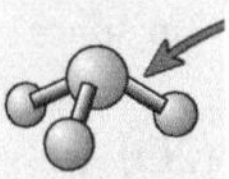

doesn't show

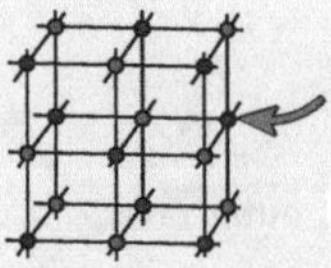

not ,
has
.

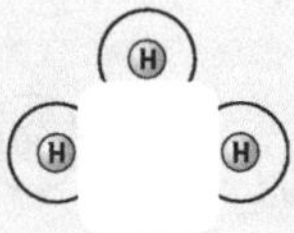

Dot and cross diagrams —

H
|
H—N—H

Displayed formula

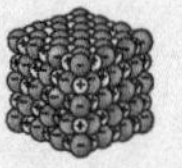

Molecular Substances

First Go: ...../...../.....

Simple Molecular Substances

COVALENT BOND — a ______ pair of electrons between two ______.

______ are made up of molecules containing a few ______.

Elements

______ (H_2)

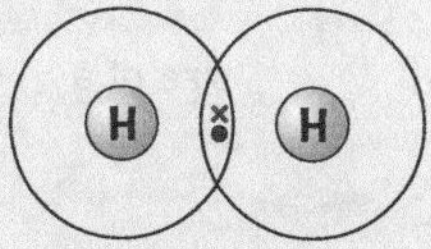

______

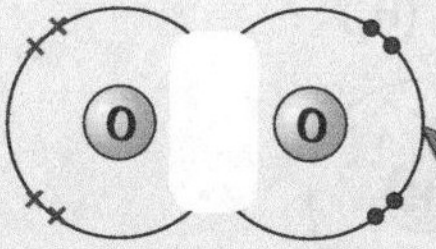

size of a ______ is around 10^{-10} m

Compounds

Hydrogen chloride (HCl)

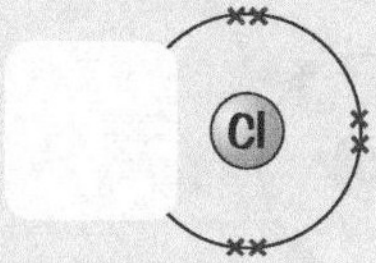

______ (CO_2)

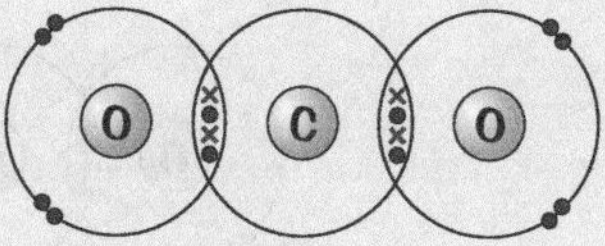

Methane ______

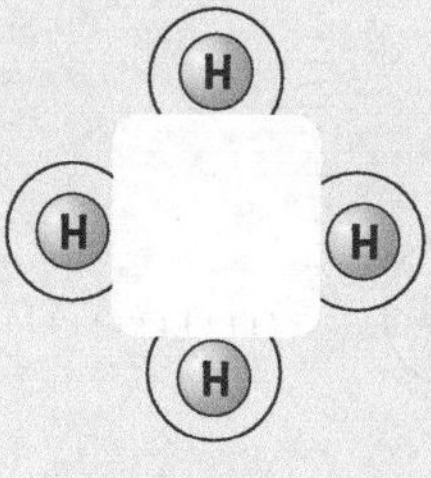

Water ______

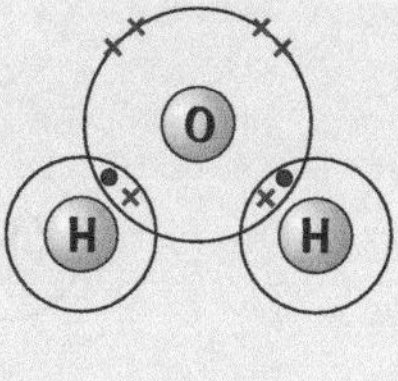

Covalent bonds between .... are .... Forces between .... are ....

Three Properties of Simple Molecular Substances

1. Low melting and boiling points — mostly ______ at ______.
2. Don't conduct electricity — there are ______ particles to ______.
3. Some are ______, and some aren't.

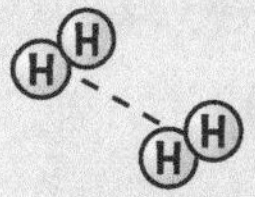

As molecules get ______, less energy is needed to ______ ______ between them.

These properties are also typical of ....

Second Go: ..... /..... /.....

Molecular Substances

Simple Molecular Substances

COVALENT BOND —

are made up of

.

Elements

(H_2)

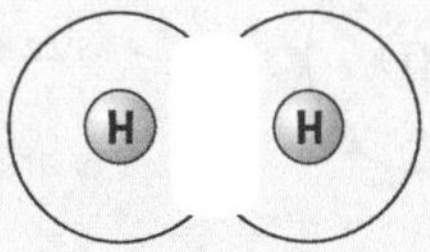

size of a

Compounds

Hydrogen chloride (HCl)

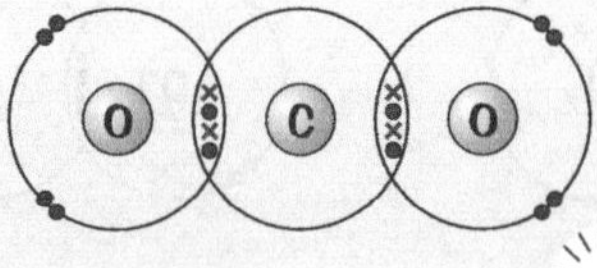

Water

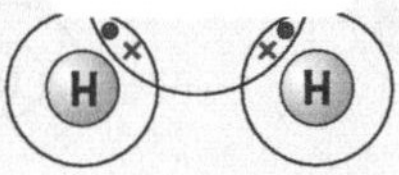

Three Properties of Simple Molecular Substances

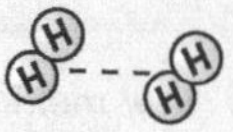

1. — mostly
   .

As molecules

, less energy is

.

2. Don't conduct

3. Some are .

These properties ....

More Covalent Substances

First Go: ..... /..... /.....

Giant Covalent Structures

GIANT COVALENT STRUCTURES — containing atoms which are by strong .

High melting and boiling points — to overcome covalent bonds.

Don't conduct (with a couple of exceptions) — no to carry charge.

in water.

Examples include .... and graphite.

Polymers

POLYMERS — very long of covalently bonded .

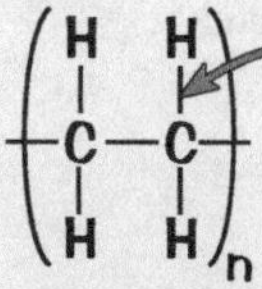

poly(ethene)

strong bonds

'n' is a large ....

Carbon Allotropes

	Diamond 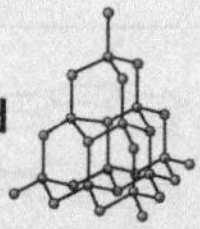	Graphite 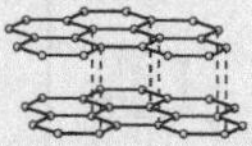	Graphene 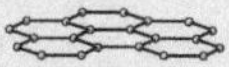
Bonding	C atoms form covalent bonds	C atoms form covalent bonds. No covalent bonds between	C atoms form covalent bonds
Properties	Very	Soft,	, light
Conductivity	Doesn't conduct	Conducts electricity and energy	electricity
Uses		, lubricant	

Each carbon atom in graphite and graphene has ....

FULLERENES — have shapes, giving them .

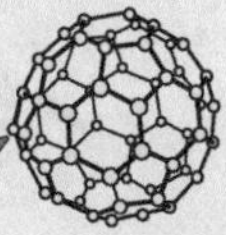

rings of (sometimes 5 or 7)

Buckminsterfullerene ( ) is .

Nanotubes are fullerenes. They have so they can conduct .

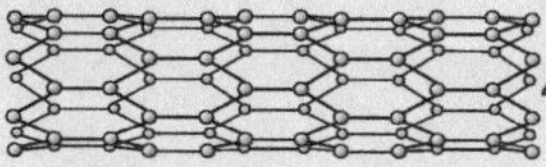

cylinder of

Second Go: ..... /..... /.....

More Covalent Substances

Giant Covalent Structures

GIANT COVALENT STRUCTURES —

High melting and

to carry charge.

Examples include

....

....

Polymers

POLYMERS —

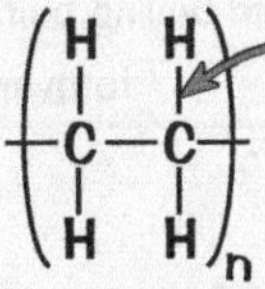

poly(ethene)

'n' is

....

....

Carbon Allotropes

	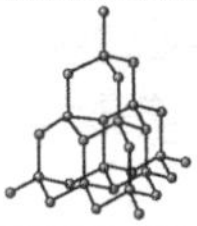	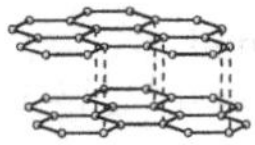	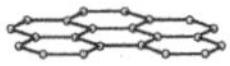
Bonding	C atoms form	C atoms form	C atoms form
Properties			
Conductivity			
Uses			

Each carbon atom in ....

— have shapes, giving them .

rings of

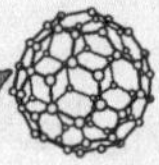

Buckminsterfullerene

.

Nanotubes .

They have

.

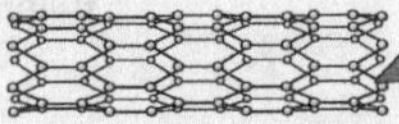

Metallic Bonding, Metals & Non-Metals

First Go: ...../...../.....

Metallic Bonding

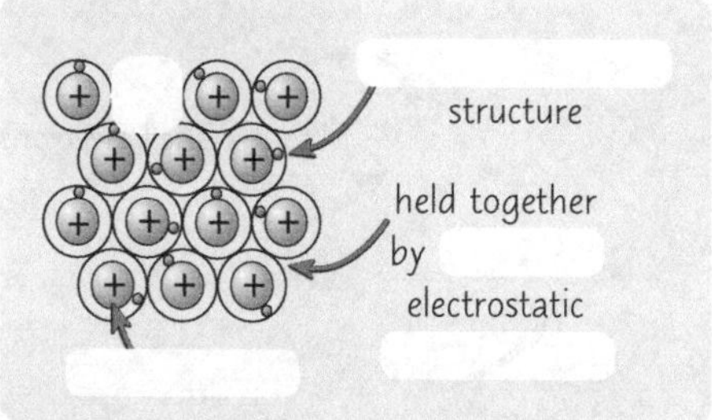

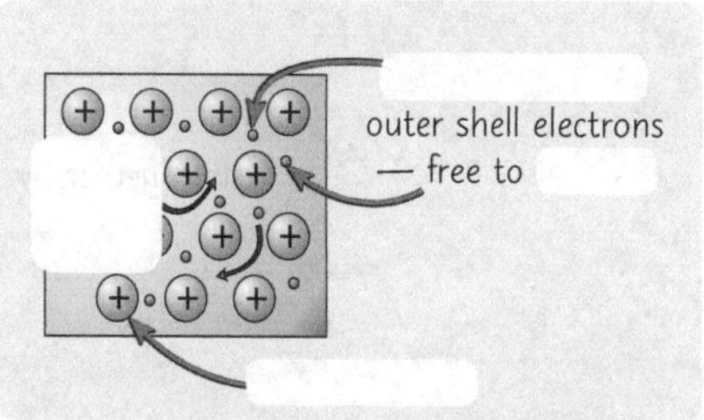

Six Properties of Metals

1. High melting and boiling points as needed to overcome . Generally at room temperature.
2. High density — ions are together.
3. Not in water.
4. appearance.
5. Good electrical conductors — .
6. Soft and malleable — layers in metals .

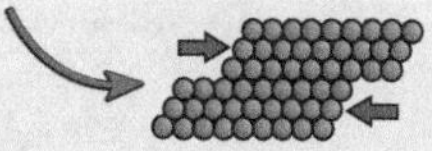

Chemical Properties of Metals and Non-Metals

METALS — outer shell , lose electrons to get .

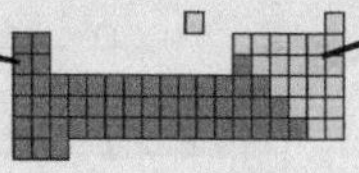

NON-METALS — outer shell , gain electrons to get .

Second Go: ...../...../.....

Metallic Bonding, Metals & Non-Metals

Metallic Bonding

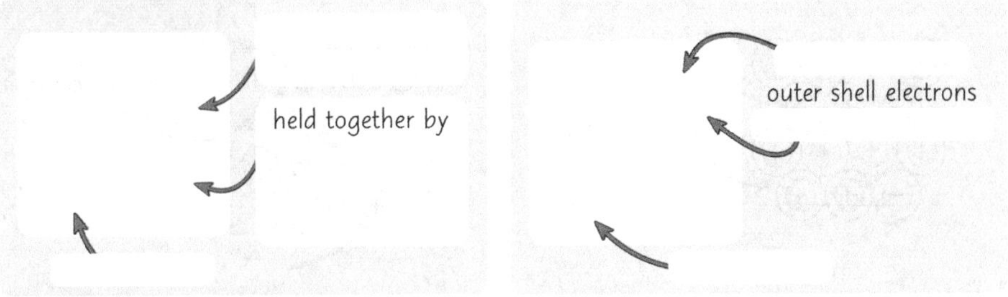

Six Properties of Metals

1. needded to overcome .
   Generally .
2. High density — .
3. in water.
4.
5. Good conductors — .
6. and malleable — .

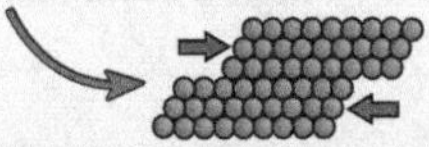

Chemical Properties of Metals and Non-Metals

METALS —

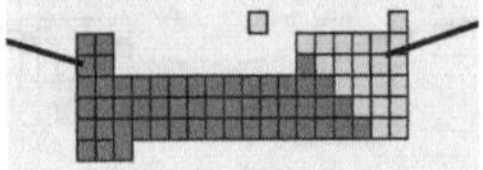

NON-METALS —

Mixed Practice Quizzes

Now, a good chemist likes to do a quiz periodically. Helpfully, here are four practice ones covering the different types of bonding from p.23-32.

Quiz 1 Date: / /

1) What is the charge on an ion of a Group 6 element? ☑
2) Why are metals malleable? ☑
3) Give one property of substances with giant covalent structures. ☑
4) How many electrons are allowed in the lowest energy shell of an atom? ☑
5) Why do ionic compounds have high melting and boiling points? ☑
6) How many bonds do carbon atoms form in a diamond structure? ☑
7) What happens to the outer shell electrons in metallic bonding? ☑
8) Why can simple molecular substances not conduct electricity? ☑
9) Why can graphite and graphene conduct electricity? ☑
10) What type of attraction is involved in ionic bonding? ☑

Total:

Quiz 2 Date: / /

1) What type of ion do Group 1 elements form? ☑
2) What is meant by ionic bonding? ☑
3) Describe the chemical bonding in graphite. ☑
4) In simple molecular substances, which are stronger — the covalent bonds or the forces between molecules? ☑
5) How many covalent bonds are there in a water molecule? ☑
6) Give one limitation of dot and cross diagrams. ☑
7) Describe what a polymer is. ☑
8) Do metals lose electrons or gain electrons in order to form ions? ☑
9) True or false? A compound with a name ending 'ide' will always contain oxygen. ☑
10) Give two properties of graphene. ☑

Total:

Mixed Practice Quizzes

Quiz 3

Date: ...... / ...... / ......

1) Give one example of a simple molecular substance.
2) Give two examples of giant covalent substances.
3) Give one limitation of a ball and stick diagram.
4) What states are simple molecular substances usually in at room temperature?
5) Which carbon allotrope is a single layer of covalently-bonded carbon atoms?
6) What type of molecule is poly(ethene)?
7) Give an example of a use for: a) diamond b) graphite
8) What is an ion?
9) What type of structure do ionic compounds have?
10) True or false? Metals usually react by losing electrons to get a full outer shell.

Total:

Quiz 4

Date: ...... / ...... / ......

1) Name one carbon allotrope that does not conduct electricity.
2) How many electrons are shared between the two atoms in an oxygen molecule?
3) Do non-metals form positive ions or negative ions?
4) How many electrons are allowed in the second electron shell of an atom?
5) Give two properties of metals.
6) In which states will ionic compounds conduct electricity?
7) What type of bonding occurs in sodium chloride?
8) Describe the electrical conductivity of a typical non-metal element.
9) Give one limitation of using a 3D model to represent an ionic structure.
10) What is the overall charge of an ionic compound?

Total:

Mass, Moles and Limiting Reactants

First Go: ..... /..... /.....

Relative Formula Mass

RELATIVE FORMULA MASS (____) — sum of ______________ of the atoms in the ______________.

The Mole

One ______ = 6.02 × 10^{23} ______ of a substance.

This is the ______________.

The .... could be e.g. ...., ... or ions.

Mass in ______________ of atoms of an element = the ____ of the element.

Mass in ______________ of molecules of a compound = the ____ of the compound.

Number of moles (____) = ______

Number of particles = moles × ______

To find the .... in a given mass, first find the ....

Balancing Equations Using Masses

If you know .... of reactants and products:

Divide ______ by ____ to find the ______________ of each substance.

↓

Divide each ______________ by the ______________.

↓

If results aren't all ______________, multiply them by ______________ so that they are ______.

↓

Put these numbers ______________ ______________.

Limiting Reactants

LIMITING REACTANT — a reactant that gets ______________ in a reaction, so ______________ ______________.

All the other reactants are ______.

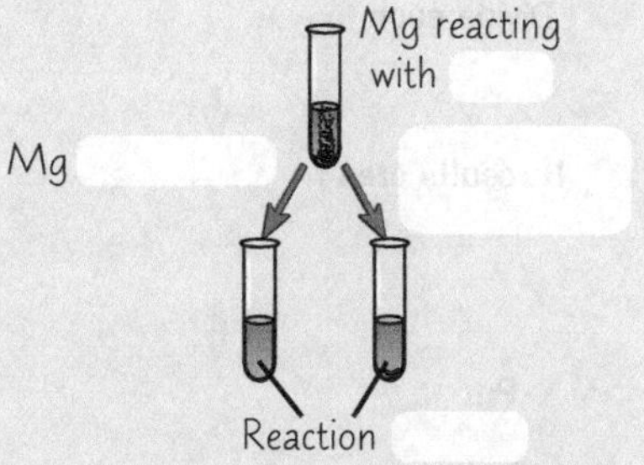

Second Go: ...../...../.....

Mass, Moles and Limiting Reactants

Relative Formula Mass

RELATIVE FORMULA MASS

The Mole

= of a substance.

Mass in
= .

Mass in
= .

Number of moles ( ) =

Number of particles =

To find the ....
.............................., first find the
....

Balancing Equations Using Masses

If you know ....
....:

Divide each

If results aren't

Put

Limiting Reactants

LIMITING REACTANT —

All the

Mg reacting with

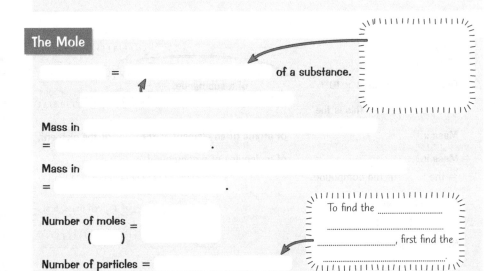

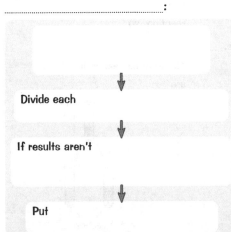

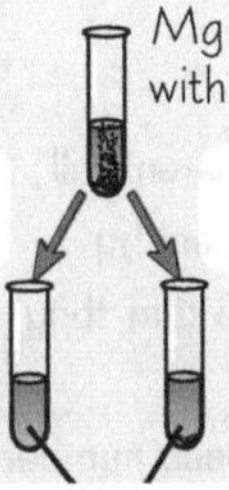

Concentration & Empirical Formulas

First Go: ..... /..... /.....

Concentration

CONCENTRATION — amount of ______ dissolved in a certain ______.

Increase the...	Concentration...
...amount of ______	
...volume of ______	

$$\text{Concentration} = \frac{\_\_\_\_\ \text{of solute}}{\_\_\_\_\ \text{of solution}}$$

Units = ___ dm^{-3}

Empirical Formula

EMPIRICAL FORMULA — the smallest ______ of atoms in a ______.

molecular formula $C_6H_{12}O_6$ ⟷ ______ formula CH_2O

To find ______ from empirical formula:

Find M_r of ______.

↓

Divide ______ by M_r of empirical formula.

↓

______ empirical formula by result.

Empirical Formula Experiment

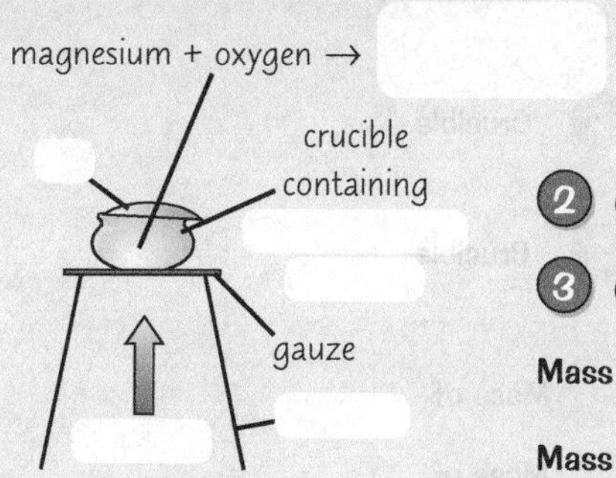

You need to weigh:

1. ______ and its lid.
2. Crucible, lid and contents ______.
3. Crucible, lid and contents ______.

Mass of ______ = 2 – 1

Mass of ______ = 3 – 2

This method .... if you know how much of each .... is present.

Use the mass of ______ ______ to work out empirical formula:

______ of each element by its A_r. → Divide each result by smallest ______ to get smallest ______ ______. → This gives the ______ ______ ______ in empirical formula.

Second Go: ...../...../.....

Concentration & Empirical Formulas

Concentration

CONCENTRATION —

Increase the...	Concentration...

Concentration = ______

Units =

Empirical Formula

EMPIRICAL FORMULA —

formula formula

$C_6H_{12}O_6$ ⟷ **CH_2O**

To find

:

Find .

↓

Divide by M_r of .

↓

Empirical Formula Experiment

magnesium + oxygen →

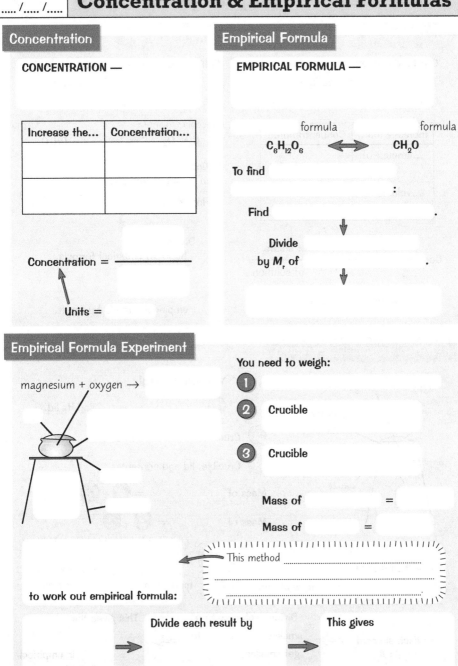

to work out empirical formula:

This method ....
....
....

You need to weigh:

1.
2. **Crucible**
3. **Crucible**

Mass of =

Mass of =

→ **Divide each result by** → **This gives**

Equations and Conservation of Mass

First Go: ..... /..... /.....

Calculating Masses Using Balanced Equations

To work out the mass of product formed from :

Write a equation for the reaction.

↓

Divide of the reactant by to find the .

↓

Use the equation to find the .

↓

Multiply this by the to work out its mass.

You can also find the mass of a .... from the mass of a .... using this method.

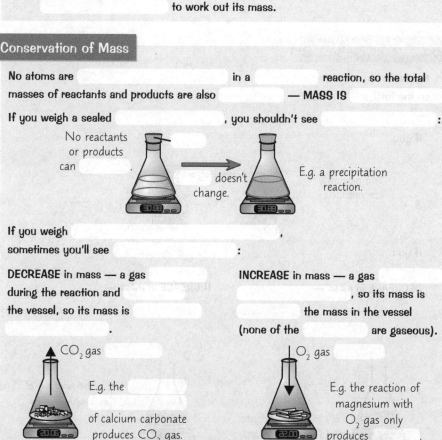

Conservation of Mass

No atoms are in a reaction, so the total masses of reactants and products are also — **MASS IS** .

If you weigh a sealed , you shouldn't see :

No reactants or products can .

E.g. a precipitation reaction.

If you weigh , sometimes you'll see :

DECREASE in mass — a gas during the reaction and the vessel, so its mass is .

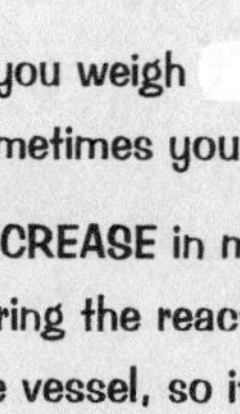

E.g. the of calcium carbonate produces CO_2 gas.

INCREASE in mass — a gas , so its mass is the mass in the vessel (none of the are gaseous).

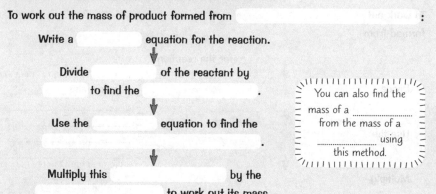

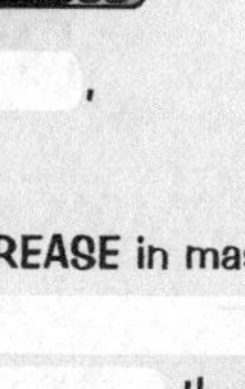

E.g. the reaction of magnesium with O_2 gas only produces .

Second Go: ...../...../.....

Equations and Conservation of Mass

Calculating Masses Using Balanced Equations

To work out

formed from :

for the reaction.

Divide

Use the

Multiply

You can also ....

....

....

....

Conservation of Mass

No atoms are ,

so the total

— .

If you

No reactants or products .

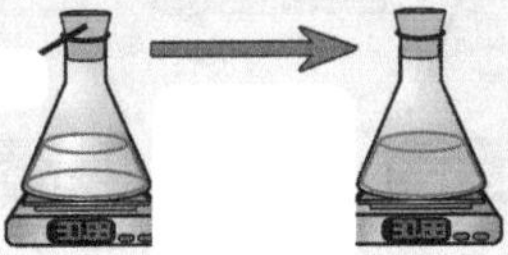

E.g. a reaction.

If you

DECREASE in mass —

INCREASE in mass —

E.g. the of calcium carbonate produces gas.

E.g. the reaction of magnesium with gas only .

Mixed Practice Quizzes

It's time for a few (well forty to be precise) questions to test what you've covered on p.35-40. Mark each test yourself to check how brilliantly you've done.

Quiz 1

Date: ...... / ...... / ......

1) Give a definition of the term 'concentration'.
2) What name is given to the reactant that's completely used up in a reaction?
3) What is the definition of 'relative formula mass'?
4) Why might the mass of a reaction vessel decrease during a reaction?
5) What is meant by the 'empirical formula' of a compound?
6) True or false? One mole of a substance contains 6.03×10^{22} particles.
7) True or false? If a reaction takes place in a sealed reaction vessel, the mass of the vessel and contents will stay the same.
8) What formula links mass in grams, moles and M_r?
9) How can you find the mass of product formed from a given mass of reactant?
10) True or false? A mole of a substance always has the same number of atoms.

Total:

Quiz 2

Date: ...... / ...... / ......

1) How many particles are in one mole of a substance?
2) What happens to a reaction when the limiting reactant has been completely used up?
3) How can an empirical formula be used to work out a molecular formula?
4) What does the M_r of a molecule tell you about one mole of that molecule?
5) Give a unit of concentration.
6) How does increasing the amount of solute affect the concentration of a solution?
7) True or false? Atoms can be destroyed in a chemical reaction.
8) Describe an experiment used to work out the empirical formula of a compound.
9) What's the relationship between the Avogadro constant and moles?
10) Suggest why the mass of a reaction vessel might increase during a reaction.

Total:

Mixed Practice Quizzes

Quiz 3

Date: ...... / ...... / ......

1) What quantity is the mass in grams of one mole of atoms of an element?
2) Which term is given to the amount of substance dissolved in a certain volume of solution?
3) How do the total masses of reactants and products in a reaction compare?
4) How do you balance an equation using the masses of reactants and products?
5) How is the number of particles in a given mass of a substance calculated?
6) What does the A_r of an element tell you about one mole of that element?
7) What is a limiting reactant?
8) How could you work out the empirical formula of magnesium oxide using the mass of Mg that reacted and the mass of magnesium oxide formed?
9) What is the Avogadro constant?
10) What term is given to the sum of the relative atomic masses in a formula?

Total:

Quiz 4

Date: ...... / ...... / ......

1) What term describes the reactants in a reaction that aren't limiting?
2) What is the term for the simplest ratio of atoms in a compound?
3) True or false? The mass of all the products of a reaction is always equal to the mass of all the reactants.
4) True or false? To find the number of particles in a sample, you should multiply the mass of the sample by the Avogadro constant.
5) How is concentration calculated from volume of solution and mass of solute?
6) How do you calculate the relative formula mass of a compound?
7) How would the mass of a reaction vessel change if a gaseous reactant from the air takes part in the reaction?
8) How does increasing the volume of a solution affect its concentration?
9) How can you use mass and M_r to find the number of moles of a substance?
10) What three things do you need to weigh when carrying out an experiment to work out the empirical formula of magnesium oxide?

Total:

States of Matter

First Go: ...../...../.....

Particle Model

	Solid		Gas
Particle Diagram			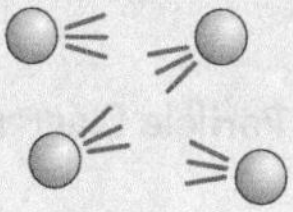
Particle Arrangement			Random
Particle Movement	Fixed position, can ______.		Move ______ in all ______.
Relative Energy of Particles	Low		

Changes of State

The change from liquid to gas at the .... is called ....

Changes between states of matter are ______ changes.

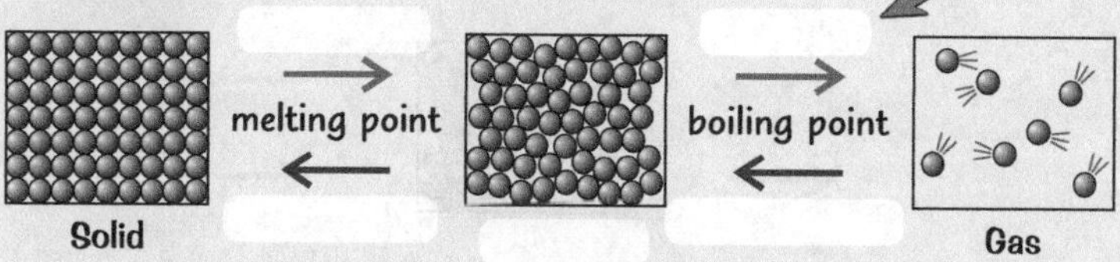

Melting and boiling point data can be used to predict a substance's ....

Melting and Boiling:

______ heats up → Particles gain ______ → Forces between particles ______ → ______ break free from ______

Condensing and Freezing:

______ cools down → Particles lose ______ → Forces between particles ______ → ______ held in ______

Chemical Changes

Chemical changes happen in ______.

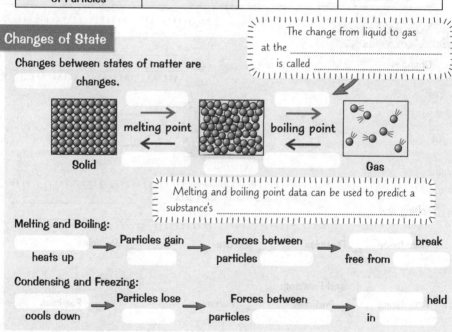

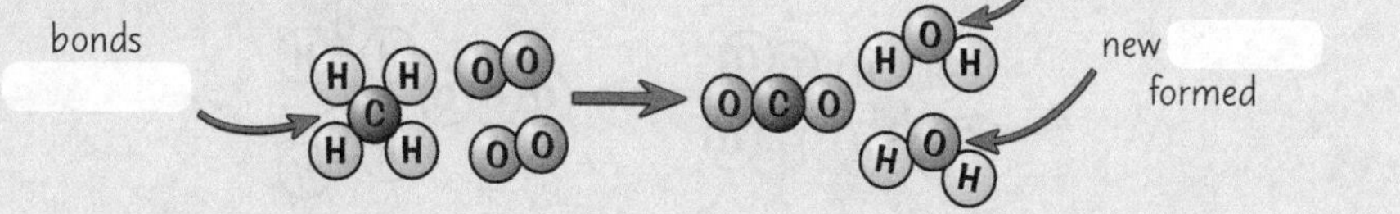

Second Go: ...../...../.....

States of Matter

Particle Model

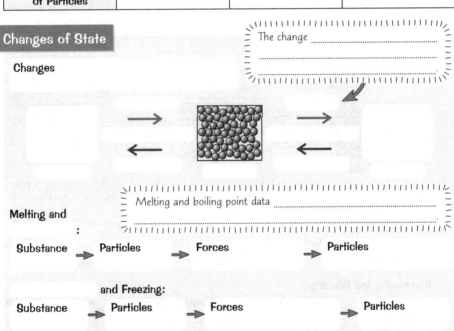

Particle Diagram		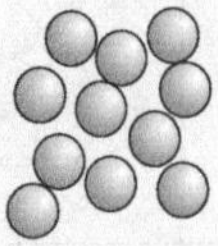	
Particle Arrangement			
Particle Movement			
Relative Energy of Particles			

Changes of State

The change ....
....
....

Changes

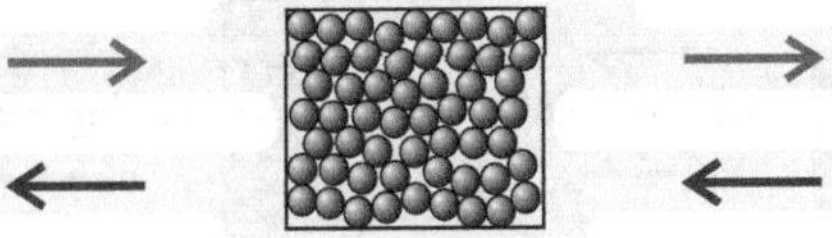

Melting and boiling point data ....
....

Melting and

:

Substance → Particles → Forces → Particles

and Freezing:

Substance → Particles → Forces → Particles

Chemical Changes

Chemical changes .

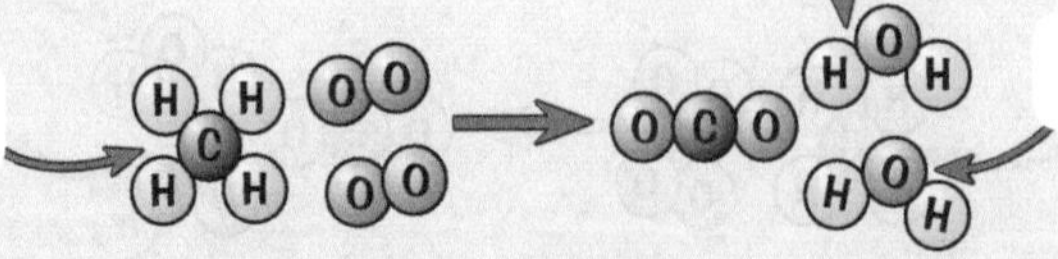

Purity

First Go: ..... /..... /.....

Definitions of Purity

	Everyday Definition	Chemical Definition
PURE SUBSTANCE	_____ or _____.	A substance containing _____ element or _____.

Pure Substances

A chemically pure substance will:

Have a _____ melting point.

Have a _____ _____ point.

You can measure _____ of a substance using _____, or with _____.

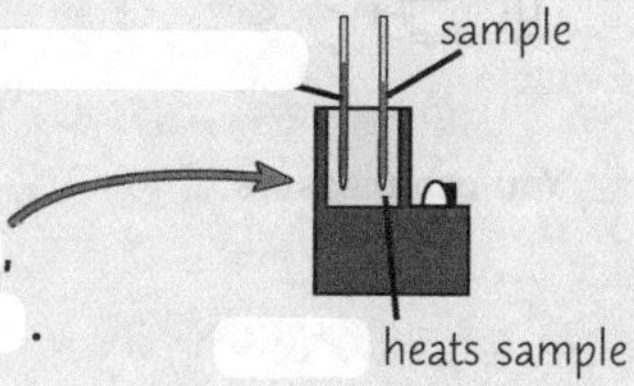

Mixtures

MIXTURES — substances made up of different _____ or compounds that _____ to each other.

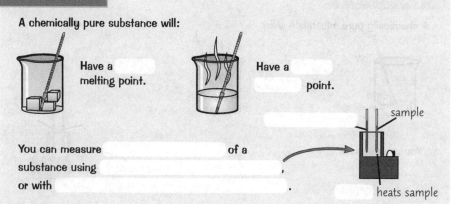

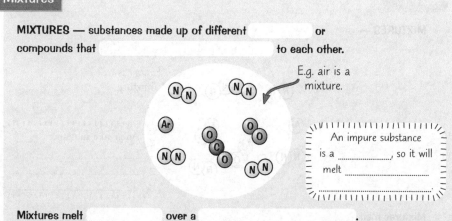

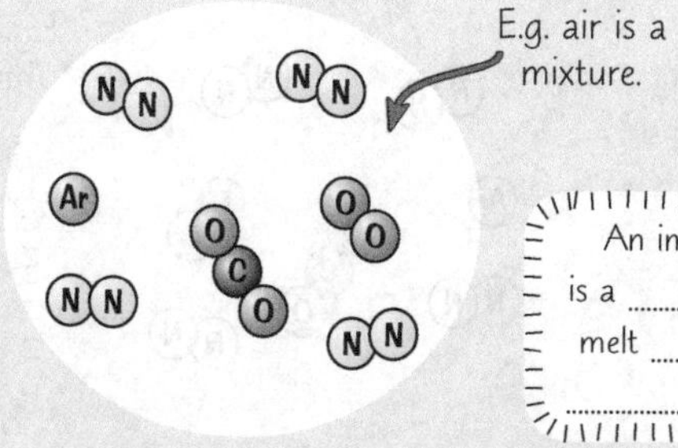

An impure substance is a ...., so it will melt ....

Mixtures melt _____ over a _____.

Second Go:
...../...../.....

Purity

Definitions of Purity

	Everyday Definition	Chemical Definition
PURE SUBSTANCE		

Pure Substances

A chemically pure substance will:

You can measure

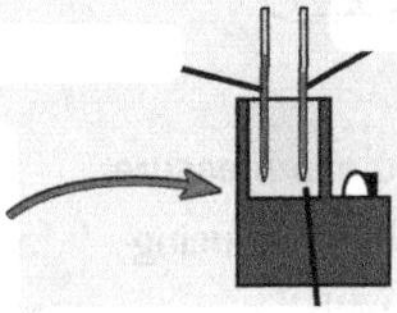

Mixtures

MIXTURES —

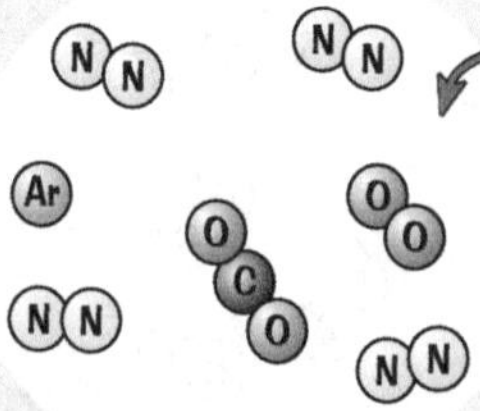

E.g. air is a mixture.

An impure substance ....
....
....
....

Mixtures melt .

Separation Techniques

First Go: ...../...../.....

Filtration

FILTRATION — separates ______ from liquids and ______.

It can be used to separate out ______, or ______ by removing ______.

Evaporation

EVAPORATION — separates ______ from solution.

Crystallisation

CRYSTALLISATION — also separates ______ from solution.

Heat solution, but ______ when ______ start to form.

↓

______ form as solution cools.

↓

Filter out ______ and leave to ______.

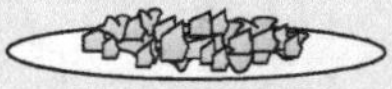

Two Types of Distillation

1 Simple distillation

.... can't separate liquids with ...., but fractional distillation can.

2 Fractional distillation

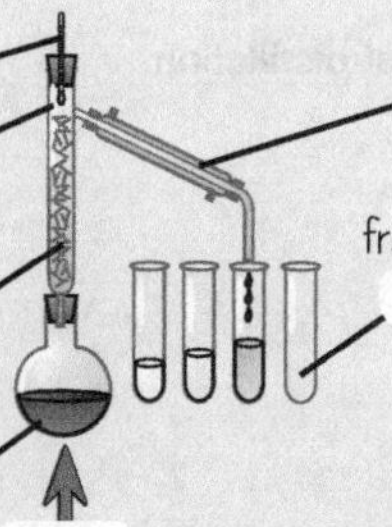

Second Go: ..... /..... /.....

Separation Techniques

Filtration

FILTRATION —

It can be used

Evaporation

EVAPORATION —

solution.

Crystallisation

CRYSTALLISATION —

Two Types of Distillation

1. **Simple distillation**

The part with the

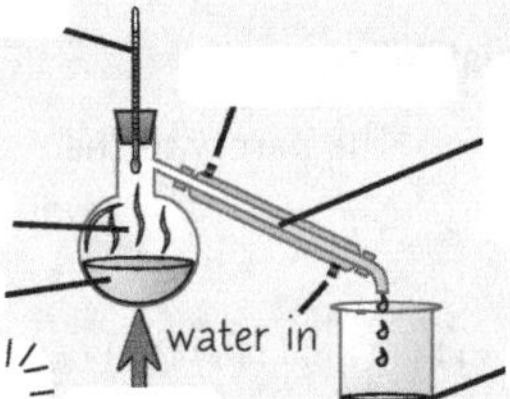

2. **Fractional distillation**

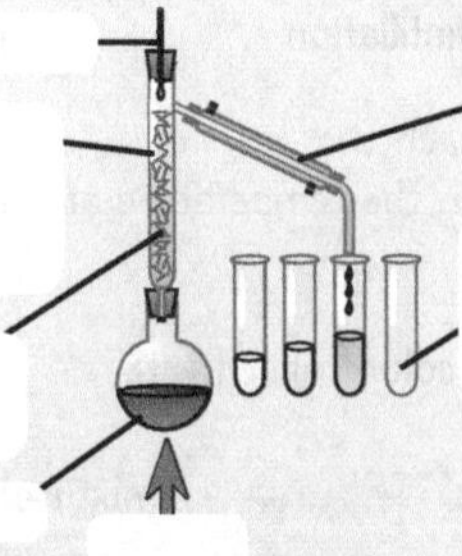

Chromatography

First Go: ...../...../.....

Paper Chromatography

CHROMATOGRAPHY — a method used to separate a ______ of ______.

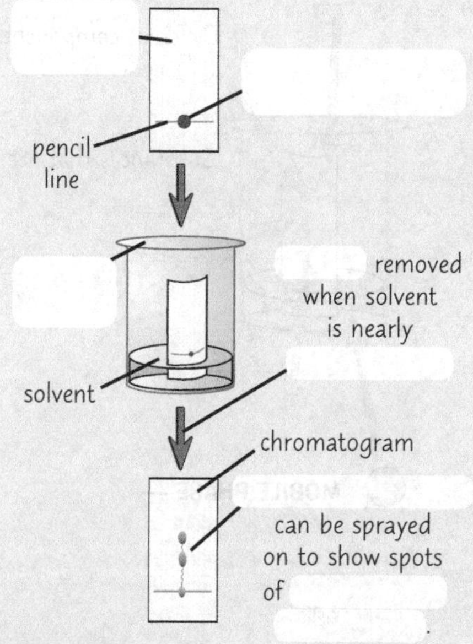

Two Phases of Chromatography

1. **STATIONARY PHASE — where the molecules ______.**
   e.g. ______ paper

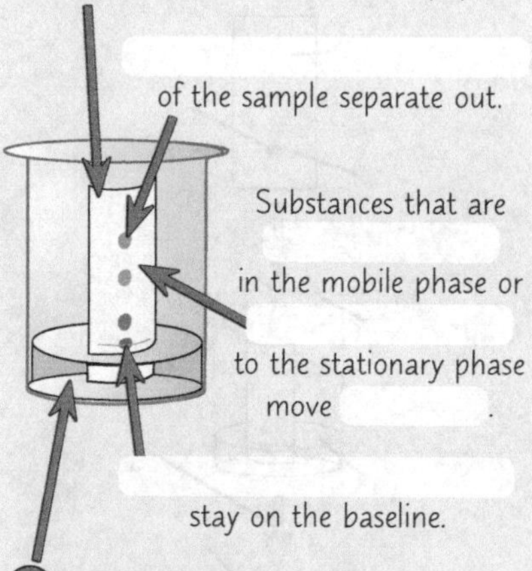

2. **MOBILE PHASE — where the molecules ______ (the ______).**
   e.g. ______ or ethanol

R_f Values

R_f VALUE — the ______ between the distance travelled by the ______ and the distance travelled by the ______.

$$R_f = \frac{\text{distance travelled by ______ (B)}}{\text{distance travelled by ______ (A)}}$$

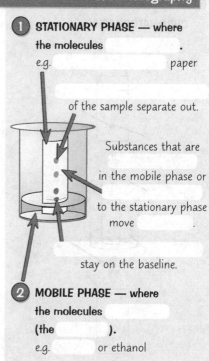

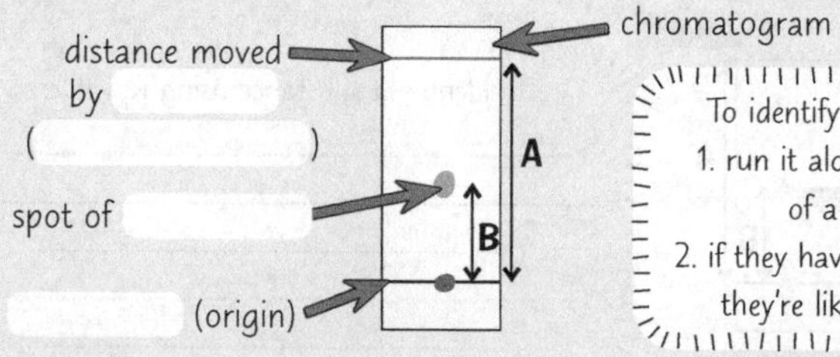

To identify a substance using R_f value:

1. run it alongside a .... of a .... substance,
2. if they have ...., they're likely the .... substance.

Chromatography can be used for ______. Pure substances won't ______ — they move as ______.

Second Go:
...../...../.....

Chromatography

Paper Chromatography

CHROMATOGRAPHY —

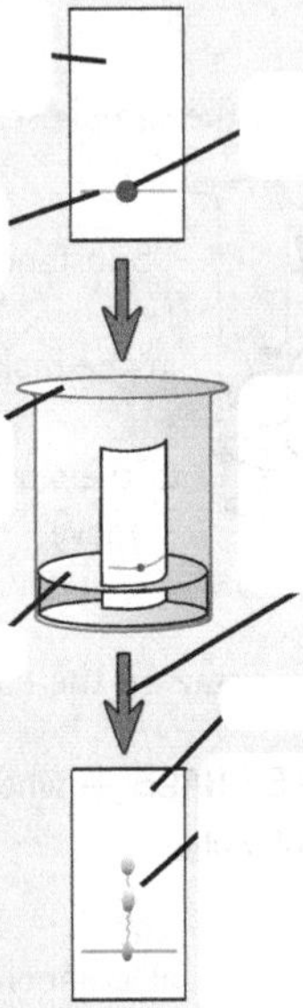

Two Phases of Chromatography

1 STATIONARY PHASE —

e.g.

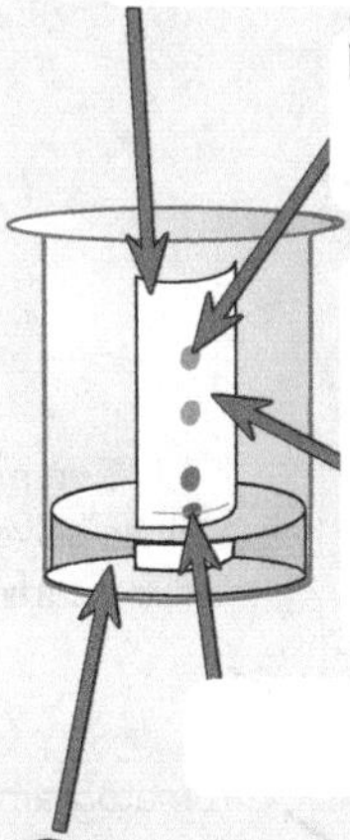

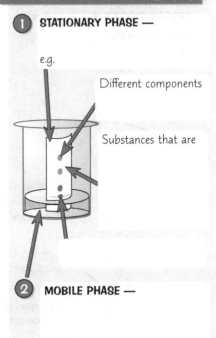

2 MOBILE PHASE —

e.g.

R_f Values

R_f VALUE —

R_f =

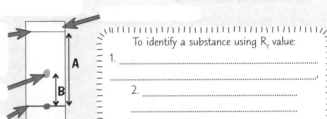

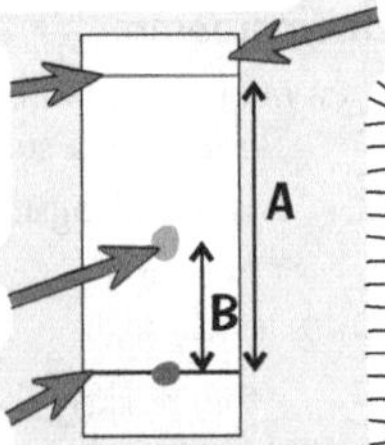

To identify a substance using R_f value:

1. ....
....,
2. ....
....
....

Chromatography can be used

Water Treatment

First Go: ..... / ..... / .....

Sources of Water

POTABLE WATER — .

Type of Water	Source
Ground water	
	Sea water
	Water .... by a human process, e.g. ....

Potable water is not .... It can contain low levels of .... and ....

Treating Water

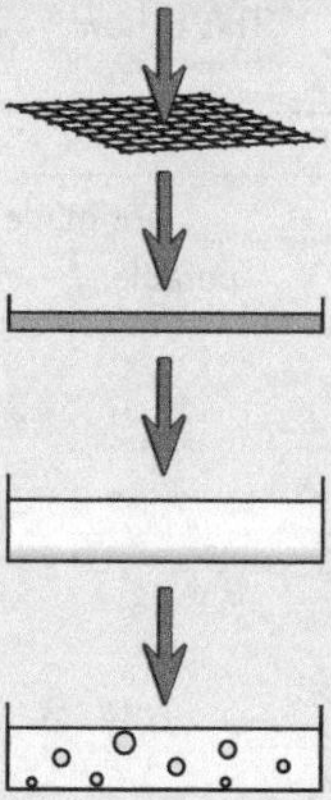

— removes any large debris such as .

filtration

— removes any smaller .

— added to water, making clump together and settle at bottom.

Chlorination

— bubbled through to kill and .

This is how .... are made potable.

Distilling Sea Water

Sea water is in areas without much to make it .

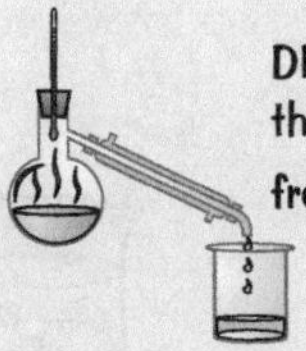

DISTILLATION — the water to separate it from .

This uses ....

Water for Analysis

Tap water has in it that can .

Water used for should be .

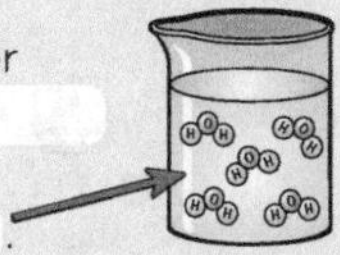

Second Go:
...../...../.....

Water Treatment

Sources of Water

Potable water is .... It can contain ....

POTABLE WATER — .

Type of Water	Source
Ground water	

Treating Water

This is how .... are made potable.

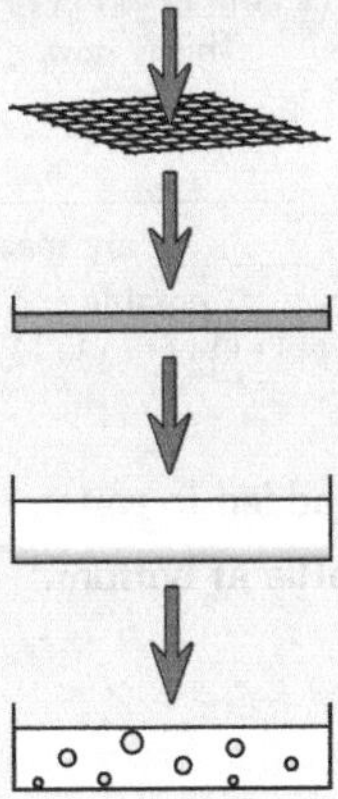

— removes .

— removes .

Chlorination —

Distilling Sea Water

Sea water is

DISTILLATION —

This uses ....

Water for Analysis

Tap water

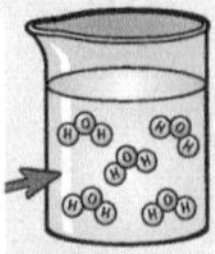

Mixed Practice Quizzes

That's a lot of facts to remember. Luckily for you, there's a handy set of quizzes here to test how much you've remembered from p.43-52.

Quiz 1

Date: ...... / ...... / ......

1) What is the chemical definition of a mixture?
2) How can the R_f value of a substance in a particular solvent be calculated?
3) What type of mixture can crystallisation be used to separate?
4) Which state of matter contains a regular arrangement of particles?
5) How many spots are formed by a pure substance during chromatography?
6) Describe the movement of particles in a gas.
7) In paper chromatography, what happens to the components of a mixture that are insoluble in the solvent being used?
8) What does the term 'pure' mean in everyday use?
9) Which technique could you use to separate an insoluble solid from a solution?
10) What is meant by 'potable water'?

Total:

Quiz 2

Date: ...... / ...... / ......

1) Which type of distillation can be used to separate liquids with similar boiling points?
2) Which states of matter does a substance change between when it boils?
3) Why should water that's used in analysis be deionised?
4) Describe the arrangement of particles in a liquid.
5) Describe the difference between the melting point of a chemically pure substance and that of a mixture.
6) Describe how you could use R_f values to identify an unknown substance.
7) What should you do after filtering out the crystals formed in crystallisation?
8) True or false? The particles gain energy when a substance freezes.
9) What name is given to the transition from liquid to solid?
10) Describe the purpose of the chlorination stage of water treatment.

Total:

Mixed Practice Quizzes

Quiz 3

Date: ...... / ...... / ......

1) Compare the relative energy of particles in solids, liquids and gases.
2) True or false? A chemically pure substance has a sharp melting point.
3) What is the definition of an R_f value?
4) Name a substance that can be used as the mobile phase in chromatography.
5) Which two changes of state involve a substance losing energy?
6) Describe how to form crystals of a salt from its solution using evaporation.
7) Is potable water chemically pure?
8) Which state of matter contains vibrating particles that are fixed in position?
9) What happens to the particles when a substance melts?
10) At what point should the filter paper be removed from the solvent when carrying out paper chromatography?

Total:

Quiz 4

Date: ...... / ...... / ......

1) When a substance condenses, do the particles gain energy or lose energy?
2) Name a technique that can be used to separate a soluble solid from a solution.
3) What is the chemical definition of a pure substance?
4) Name a process that is used to make potable water from sea water.
5) In chromatography, what does the amount of separation of the different components in a sample depend on?
6) How are small solids removed from ground water?
7) Which part of a mixture of liquids will evaporate first in simple distillation?
8) What process occurs when a substance goes from a solid to a liquid?
9) Is freezing an example of a physical change or a chemical change?
10) Which state of matter consists of particles that are close together but are moving round each other?

Total:

Acids and Bases

First Go: ..... /..... /.....

The pH Scale

Alkalis are .... bases.

pH 0 1 2 3 4 5 6 7 8 9 10 11 12 13 14

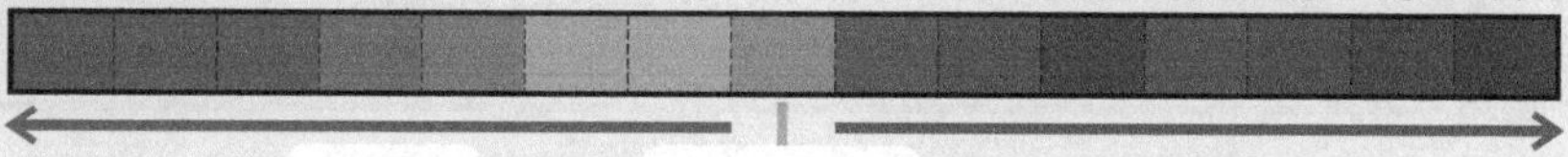

most ALKALIS most

form in water form in water

higher H^+ concentration = pH **higher OH^- concentration = pH**

Indicators

	Colour when solution is...		
	acidic	**neutral**	
	red		**blue**
methyl orange	**red**		
phenol-phthalein			**pink**

Neutralisation Reactions

.... that reacts with .... is a base.

.... **+ base → salt +** ....

The products of neutralisation reactions are .

.... **+ $OH^-_{(aq)}$ →** ....

Acid Used	Salt Produced
HCl	
H_2SO_4	
HNO_3	

Reactions of Acids

acid + metal oxide → +

acid + metal hydroxide → +

acid + **→ salt +** **+ carbon dioxide**

acid + **→** **+ hydrogen**

To test for hydrogen:

lighted

H_2 gas in

To test for carbon dioxide:

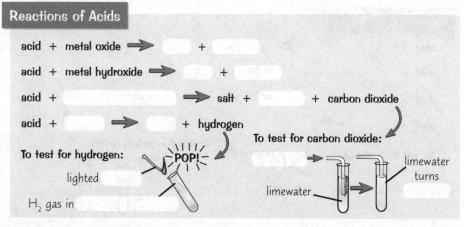

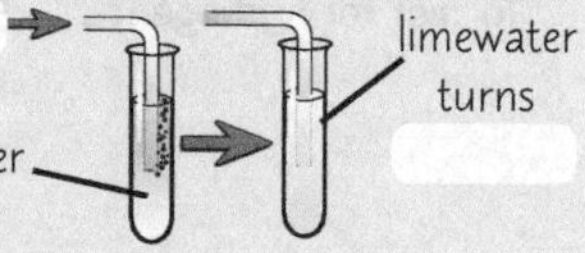

Second Go:
..... /..... /.....

Acids and Bases

The pH Scale

Alkalis are ....

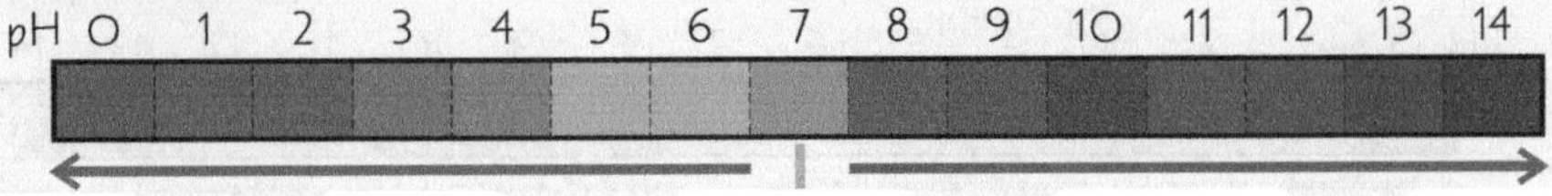

form

higher

= **pH**

form

higher

= **pH**

Indicators

	Colour when solution is...		
	acidic		
			blue
phenol-phthalein			

Neutralisation Reactions

.... that reacts with ....

.... + ... ➔ .... + ...

The products of

.

.... + ... ➔ ....

Acid Used	Salt Produced
H_2SO_4	

Reactions of Acids

acid + ➔ +

acid + ➔ +

acid + ➔ **salt** + +

acid + ➔ +

To test for hydrogen:

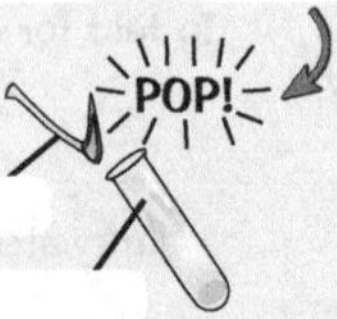

To test for carbon dioxide:

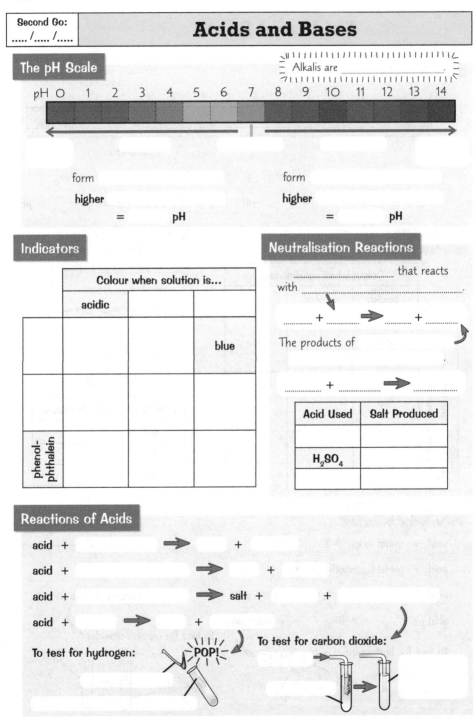

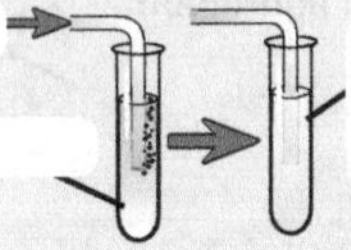

Strong and Weak Acids

First Go: ..... /..... /.....

Acid Strength

	Definition	Examples
ACID	An acid that ionises ( ) in water to produce ions. E.g. HCl →	hydrochloric acid acid acid
WEAK ACID	An acid that ( ) in water to produce ions. E.g. $CH_3COOH \rightleftharpoons$	acid citric acid acid

Strength vs Concentration

	A measure of...
ACID STRENGTH	...the proportion of that in water.
ACID CONCENTRATION	...the number of in of water.

Dilute acids have a concentration.
Concentrated acids have a concentration.

The pH will .... with increasing acid .... regardless of whether ....

pH and H^+ Ion Concentration

pH — a measure of the in a solution.

Change in concentration of solution	Change in pH of solution
increases by a factor of	by 1
decreases by a	

For a given concentration of acid, as the acid strength , pH .

Second Go: ...../...../.....	

Strong and Weak Acids

Acid Strength

STRONG ACID	Definition: E.g.	Examples:
WEAK ACID	Definition: E.g.	Examples:

Strength vs Concentration

ACID STRENGTH	A measure of...
ACID CONCENTRATION	A measure of...

Dilute acids have .

Concentrated acids have .

The pH ....
....
....

pH and H^+ Ion Concentration

pH — .

Change in	Change in

For a given

Insoluble and Soluble Salts

First Go: ..... /..... /.....

Solubility

You can use these rules to .... whether a product will be .... or ....

Substance	Soluble?
common salts of sodium, potassium and ammonium	
nitrates	
common chlorides	yes (except .... and lead chloride)
common sulfates	yes (except lead, barium and ....)
common carbonates and hydroxides	.... (except for ...., ... and ammonium ones)

Making Insoluble Salts

Making Soluble Salts

acid + insoluble base:

Excess added to acid, so .

acid + soluble base:

The acid is measured using a ....

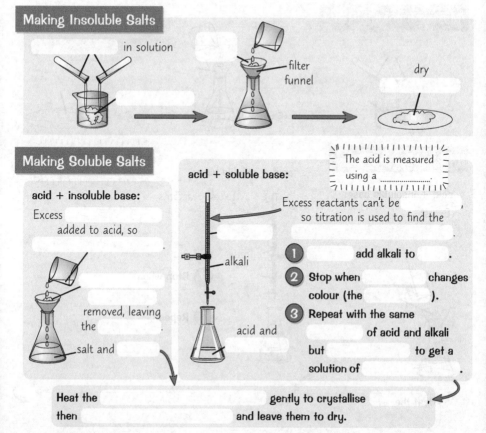

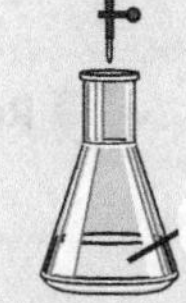

Excess reactants can't be , so titration is used to find the .

1. **add alkali to .**
2. **Stop when changes colour (the).**
3. **Repeat with the same of acid and alkali but to get a solution of .**

Heat the gently to crystallise , then and leave them to dry.

Second Go:
...../...../.....

Insoluble and Soluble Salts

Solubility

You can use these rules to predict whether a ....

Substance	Soluble?
common salts of sodium, ... and	
nitrates	
common chlorides	
common sulfates	
common carbonates and	

Making Insoluble Salts

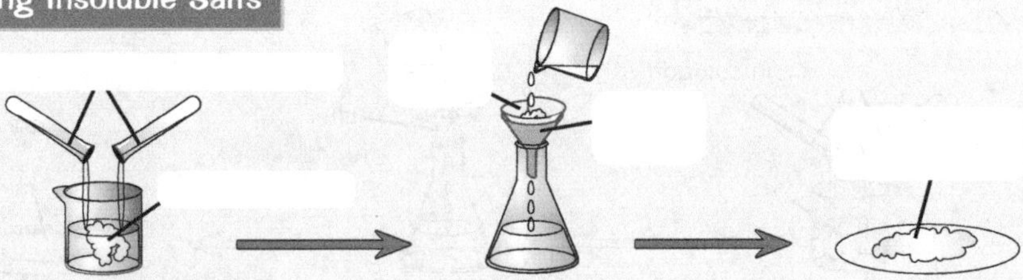

Making Soluble Salts

acid + insoluble base:

Excess

acid + soluble base:

The acid is measured using a ....

Excess reactants

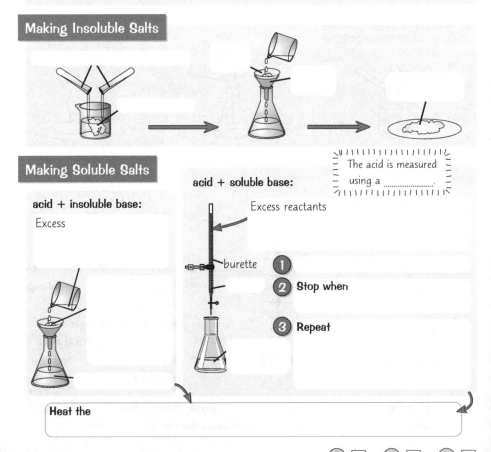

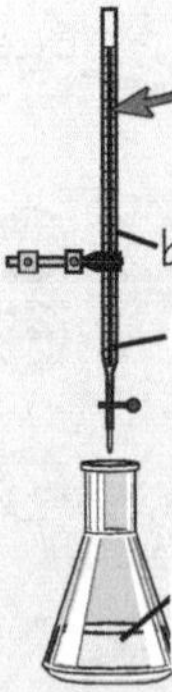

1

2 **Stop when**

3 **Repeat**

Heat the

Electrolysis

First Go: ...../...../.....

Electrochemical Cells

ELECTROLYSIS — passing an ______ through an ______, causing it to ______.

Electrolyte — a molten or dissolved ....

Electrolyte = ______ compound:

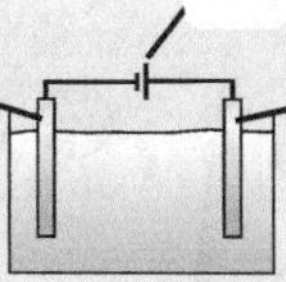

Electrolyte = ______ compound:

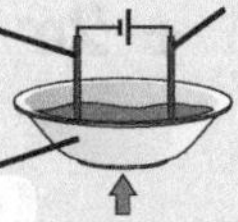

The electrodes should be .... (unreactive) — e.g. ...., platinum.

Ion	Moves to...	It is...
cation (+ve)	.... (–ve)	.... (gains e^-)
.... (–ve)	.... (+ve)	.... (loses e^-)

Half Equations

HALF EQUATIONS — show ______ ______ during reactions.

To write a half equation:

1. Write the thing being ______ ______.
2. Write the thing it is ______ ______.
3. Balance the numbers of ______.
4. Add ______ to balance the charges.

$$2H^+ + 2e^- \rightarrow H_2$$

Electrolysis of Molten Ionic Compounds

______ lead bromide ______

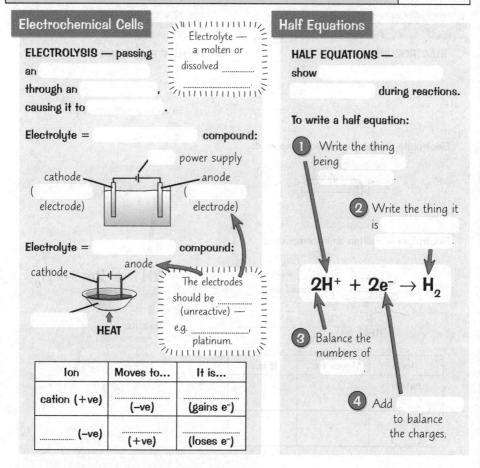

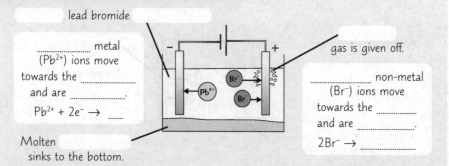

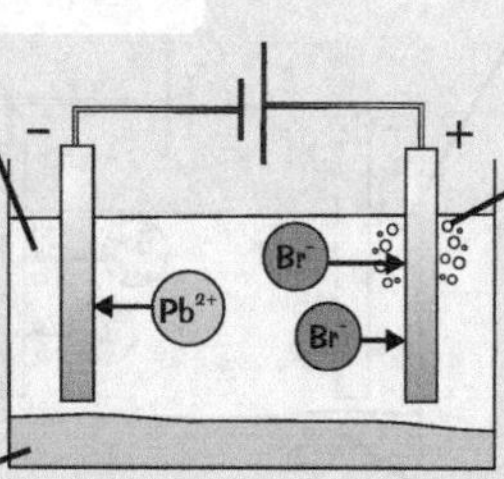

.... metal (Pb^{2+}) ions move towards the .... and are ....

$Pb^{2+} + 2e^- \rightarrow$ ....

______ gas is given off.

.... non-metal (Br^-) ions move towards the .... and are ....

$2Br^- \rightarrow$ ....

Molten ______ sinks to the bottom.

Second Go: ...../...../.....

Electrolysis

Electrochemical Cells

ELECTROLYSIS —

Electrolyte — ....

Electrolyte = dissolved ionic compound:

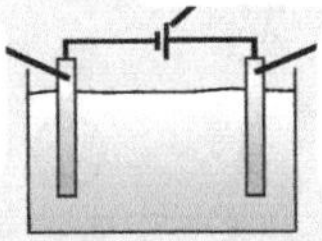

Electrolyte = molten ionic compound:

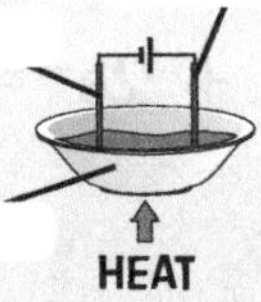

The electrodes should be ....

Ion	Moves to...	It is...
cation (..........)		
anion (..........)		

Half Equations

HALF EQUATIONS —

To write a half equation:

1. Write
2. Write
3. Balance
4. Add

$$2H^+ + 2e^- \rightarrow H_2$$

Electrolysis of Molten Ionic Compounds

Positive

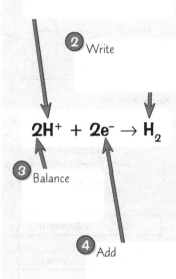

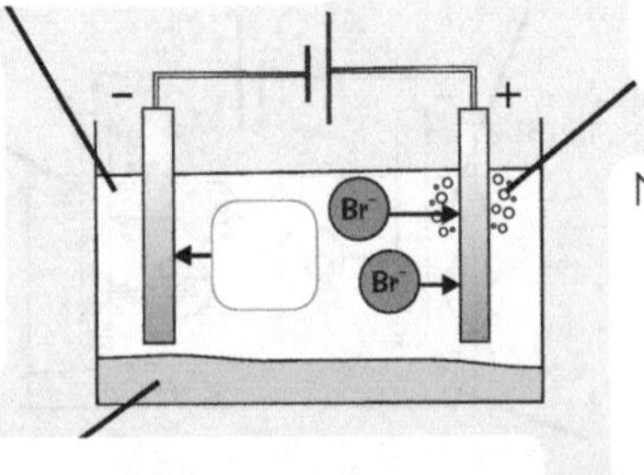

Negative

More on Electrolysis

First Go: ..... /..... /.....

Electrolysis of Aqueous Ionic Compounds

produced at if it is than H_2.

If metal is than H_2, is produced at .

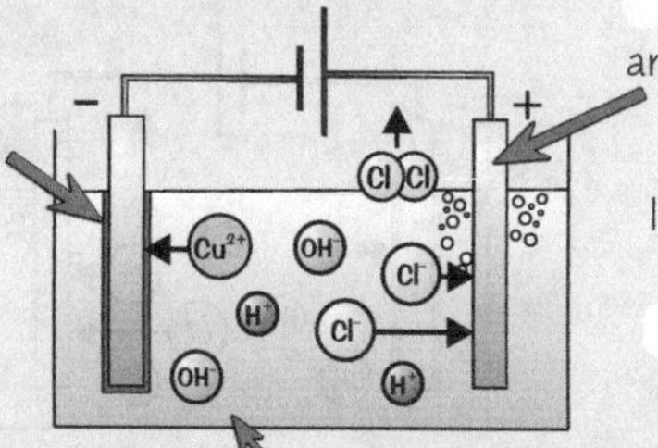

e.g. $CuCl_2$ solution

produced at anode if are present.

If are present, are produced at anode.

Aqueous Electrolyte	Product at Cathode	Product at Anode
Copper chloride	**Copper** Cu^{2+} + ... → Cu	
	Hydrogen $2H^+ + 2e^- \rightarrow$	**Chlorine** $2Cl^- \rightarrow Cl_2 + 2e^-$
Sodium sulfate Na_2SO_4		**Oxygen and water** $4OH^- \rightarrow$ .... $+ 4e^-$
Water acidified with .... H_2O/H_2SO_4		

Purifying Copper

pure

cathode

$CuSO_4$

impure

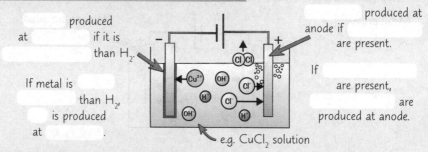

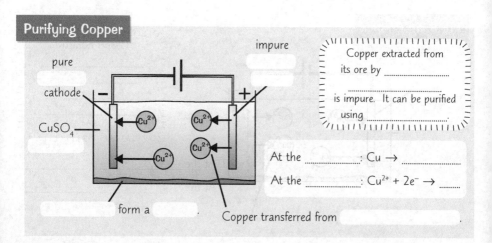

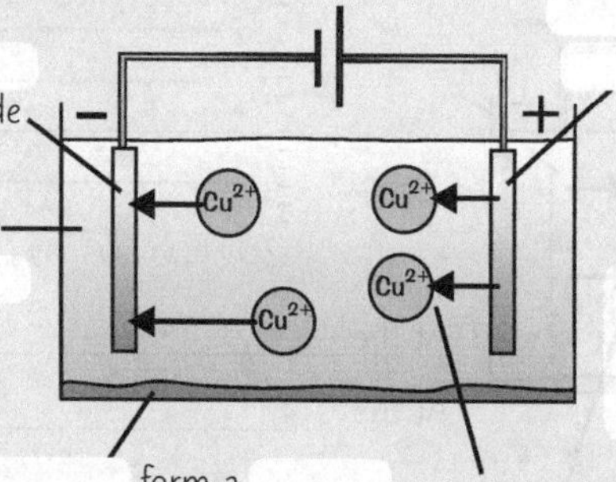

form a .

Copper transferred from .

Copper extracted from its ore by .... is impure. It can be purified using ....

At the ....: Cu → ....

At the ....: $Cu^{2+} + 2e^- \rightarrow$ ....

Second Go: ...../...../.....

More on Electrolysis

Electrolysis of Aqueous Ionic Compounds

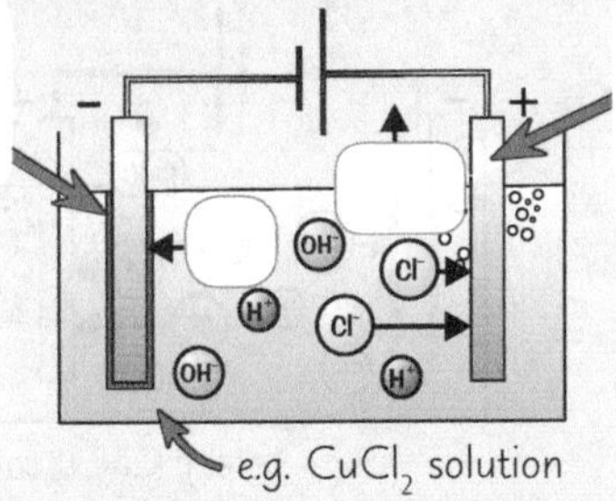

Aqueous Electrolyte	Product at Cathode	Product at Anode
Copper chloride $CuCl_2$		
Sodium chloride NaCl		
Sodium sulfate Na_2SO_4		
Water acidified with sulfuric acid H_2O/H_2SO_4		

Purifying Copper

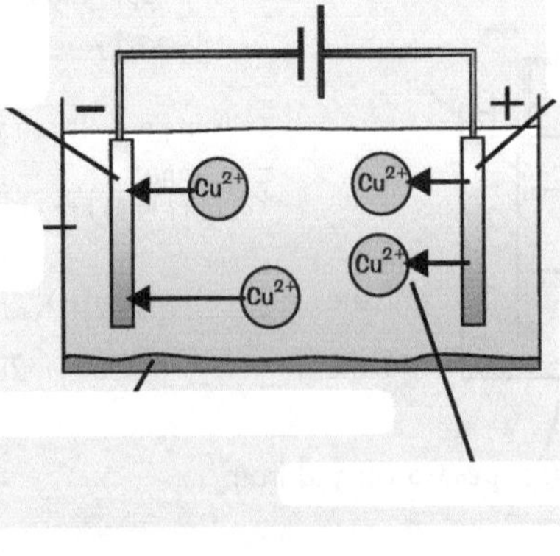

Copper extracted

....

....

....

....

....

At the ....: ....

At the ....: ....

Mixed Practice Quizzes

Wow, that's Topic 3 done already! Must be time to test yourself on p.55-64. There's plenty to remember, but I'm confident you can neutralise these quizzes.

Quiz 1

Date: ...... / ...... / ......

1) Explain what is meant by the term 'electrolysis'.
2) What ions are produced when an acid ionises in water?
3) Give the cathode half equation for the electrolysis of aqueous copper chloride.
4) What type of acid completely ionises in water?
5) True or false? All nitrate salts are soluble.
6) If the H^+ concentration of a solution increases by a factor of 10, how will the pH of the solution change?
7) Describe the set-up of an electrolysis cell that is used to purify copper.
8) Describe how you would test for the presence of carbon dioxide gas.
9) State what is meant by the term 'electrolyte'.
10) Which has a higher pH value — an acid or an alkali?

Total:

Quiz 2

Date: ...... / ...... / ......

1) Which type of salt is produced when HNO_3 reacts with a base?
2) What is acid concentration a measure of?
3) What is produced by the reaction of an acid and a metal oxide?
4) Define a weak acid.
5) How does increasing the acid concentration affect the pH of a solution?
6) Describe how the colour of a solution containing phenolphthalein changes as its pH increases from acidic to alkaline.
7) Give the general equation for a neutralisation reaction.
8) True or false? In electrolysis, metal ions are reduced at the anode.
9) What name is given to the negative electrode in electrolysis?
10) Describe a method for preparing an insoluble salt from two soluble salts.

Total:

Mixed Practice Quizzes

Quiz 3

Date: ...... / ...... / ......

1) Which electrode do cations move to during electrolysis?
2) Which ions react in a neutralisation reaction between an acid and a base?
3) Is lead chloride soluble in water?
4) Describe how to write a half equation.
5) What is acid strength a measure of?
6) What is the pH of a neutral solution?
7) How can a lighted splint be used to identify hydrogen gas?
8) What would you observe if you added methyl orange to a colourless neutral solution?
9) What gas is produced at the anode during the electrolysis of molten lead bromide?
10) Give the rule that determines what is produced at the cathode during the electrolysis of an aqueous ionic compound.

Total:

Quiz 4

Date: ...... / ...... / ......

1) How could you get dry crystals of a soluble salt from solution?
2) What method could you use to find out the exact volume of alkali required to react with a quantity of acid?
3) What can be reacted with an acid to produce carbon dioxide?
4) Which type of ion will move to the anode during electrolysis?
5) What is a base?
6) True or false? A weak acid is an acid that only partially ionises in water.
7) What name is given to a base that is soluble in water?
8) Give the anode half equation for the electrolysis of molten lead bromide.
9) Name a hydroxide salt that is soluble in water.
10) What substances are produced at the anode during the electrolysis of an aqueous ionic compound if no halide ions are present?

Total:

Reactivity of Metals

First Go: ..... /..... /.....

The Reactivity Series

- form
- Less to .

increasing reactivity ↑	Reaction with water	Reaction with dilute acid
Potassium	— forms metal and	— forms and
Magnesium	Reacts with but not — forms and	— forms salt and
Aluminium		
Zinc		Some bubbling — forms salt and
HYDROGEN		
	No reaction	
Gold		

- form .
- More to .

DISPLACEMENT REACTION — when a more reactive a less reactive in a compound.

You can use the reactions with acid and water, plus displacement reactions, to find ....

Redox Reactions

REDOX REACTION — where in a reaction is and another is .

	Gain of...	or Loss of...
Oxidation =		
Reduction =		

reactions are redox reactions.

$$Ca_{(s)} + ZnSO_{4(aq)} \rightarrow CaSO_{4(aq)} + Zn_{(s)}$$

Ca is — it electrons. Zn is — it electrons.

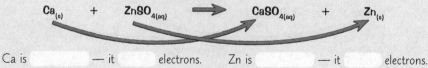

Second Go:
..... /..... /.....

Reactivity of Metals

The Reactivity Series

reactivity ↑	Reaction with water	Reaction with dilute acid
Magnesium		
Aluminium		
Zinc		
Gold		

DISPLACEMENT REACTION —

You can use the reactions ....

Redox Reactions

REDOX REACTION —

	of... or	of...
Oxidation =		
Reduction =		

are redox reactions.

$Ca_{(s)}$ + $ZnSO_{4(aq)}$ →

Ca

Zn

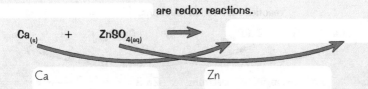

Extracting Metals

First Go: ...../...../.....

Extraction Methods

Most metals are extracted from ______ taken from ______.

- increasing reactivity ↑
- K, Na, Ca, Mg, ...: ______ — used for metals more reactive than carbon.
- ...... , Zn, Fe, Cu: Reduction using ______ — can only be used to extract ______ ______.
- Ag, Au: Found as uncombined ______.

.... requires lots of .... so is expensive — only used for ....

Heating the ore with .... it — .... is removed.

Extraction by Electrolysis

E.g. extraction of aluminium:

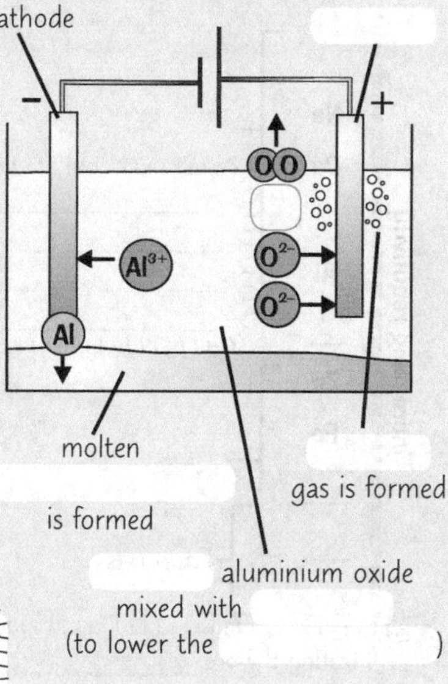

Biological Methods of Extraction

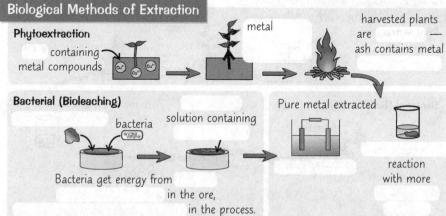

Phytoextraction

______ containing metal compounds

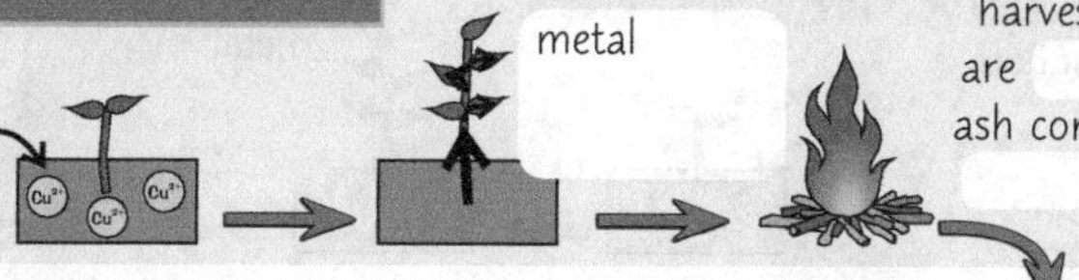

harvested plants are ______ — ash contains metal ______

Bacterial (Bioleaching) ______

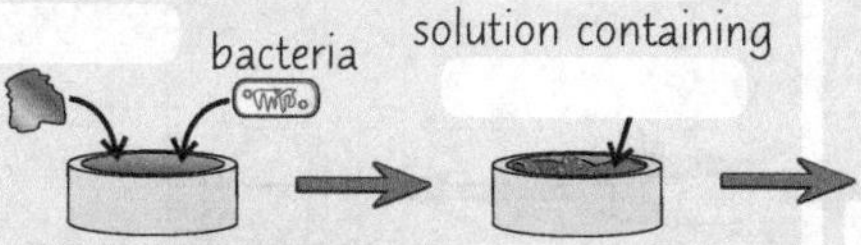

Bacteria get energy from ______ ______ in the ore, ______ in the process.

Pure metal extracted

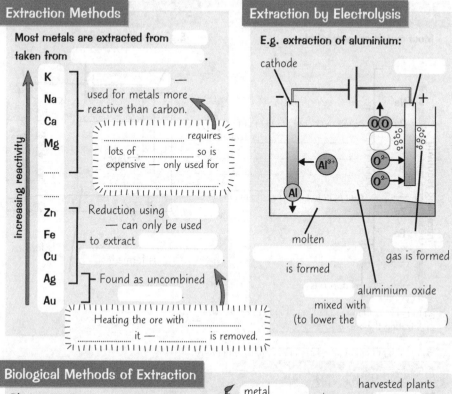

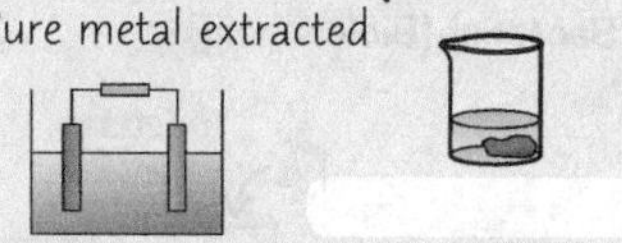

______ reaction with more ______ ______

Compared to traditional methods:

- **Can be used to extract ______ from ______.**
- **Less ______.**
- ______.

Second Go: ..... /..... /.....

Extracting Metals

Extraction Methods

Most metals are extracted

increasing reactivity

- ....
- **Na**
- **Ca**
- ....
- **Al**
- ....
- **Zn**
- **Fe**
- ....
- ....
- ....

.... requires ....

Found as ....

Heating the ore ....

Extraction by Electrolysis

E.g. extraction of aluminium:

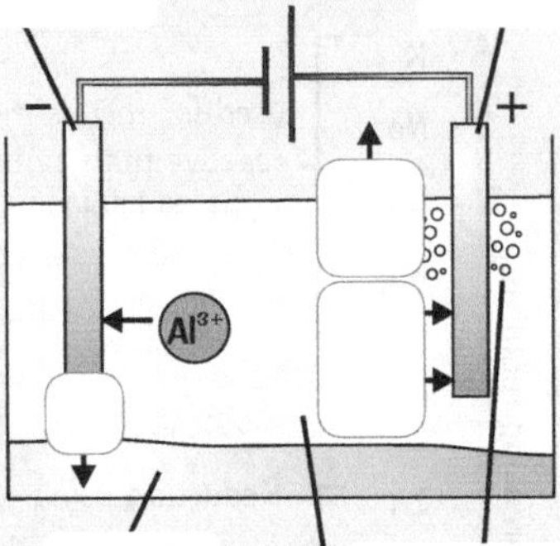

is formed

is formed

molten

Biological Methods of Extraction

Phytoextraction

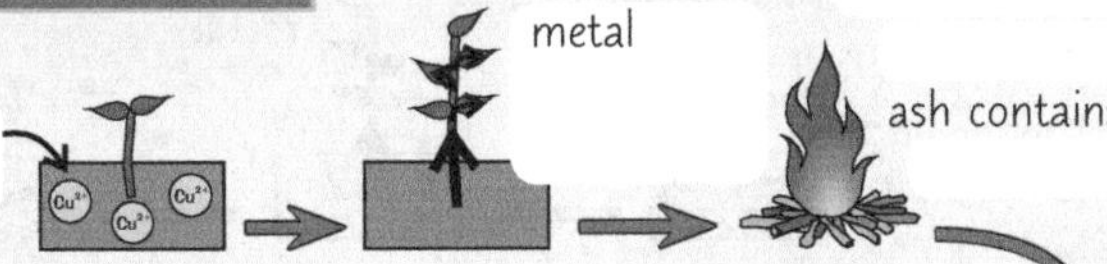

metal

—

ash contains metal

Bacterial (Bioleaching)

Pure metal extracted

Compared to traditional methods:

-
-
-

Recycling and Life Cycle Assessments

First Go: ..... /..... /.....

Issues With Extracting Metals

Metals are ______ resources — they ______ ______.

Mining metals damages ______.

Fossil fuels need ______ to provide ______ ______, causing ______.

Fossil fuels are also ...., so need to ....

Benefits of Recycling Metals

Reduces the amount of ______.

Reduces the need for ______ — preserves ______.

Uses ______ energy than ______ ______.

Often ______ to recycle than ______.

Recycling also ______.

Life Cycle Assessments

LIFE CYCLE ASSESSMENT (LCA) — an assessment of the ______ of a product over each stage of its life.

Life Cycle Assessment Stage	Considerations
....	• Metals need .... and can .... • Raw materials for .... often come from .... (..).
Manufacturing	• Uses a lot of .... and can .... • Waste products need .... • .... from manufacturing processes shouldn't be ....
Using the Product	• Could damage the environment, e.g. by releasing ...., or by contaminating ....
Product	• Disposal in .... takes up space and can cause pollution. • .... causes air pollution.

Second Go:
...../...../.....

Recycling and Life Cycle Assessments

Issues With Extracting Metals

Metals are

Fossil fuels need

Fossil fuels are ....

....

....

Benefits of Recycling Metals

Reduces the need

Uses less

Often

Recycling also

Life Cycle Assessments

LIFE CYCLE ASSESSMENT (LCA) —

Life Cycle Assessment Stage	Considerations
	• •
	• • Waste products • Polluted water
Using the Product	•
	• Disposal in landfill • Incineration

Reversible Reactions

First Go: ..... /..... /.....

Equilibrium

DYNAMIC EQUILIBRIUM — the …… …… reactions are both happening …… .

…… — where the products can react to form …… .

Equilibrium can only be reached when a …… …… takes place in a …… (where nothing can enter or leave).

$$A + B \rightleftharpoons C + D$$

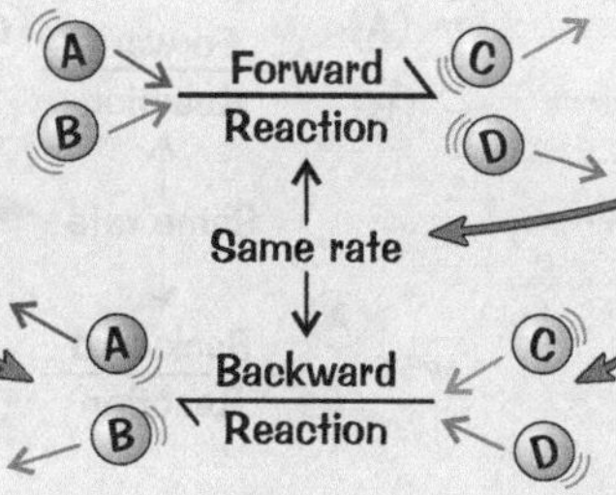

At equilibrium, the …… of reactants and products …… .

If higher concentration of …… …… : equilibrium lies to the …… .

If higher concentration of …… …… : equilibrium lies to the …… .

Haber Process

$$N_{2(g)} + 3H_{2(g)} \rightleftharpoons 2NH_{3(g)}$$

- $N_{2(g)}$ obtained from ……
- $3H_{2(g)}$ extracted from …… e.g. natural gas
- $2NH_{3(g)}$ …… produced

Conditions:

- …… °C
- …… **atmospheres**
- …… **catalyst**

Le Chatelier's Principle

If the …… of a reversible reaction at equilibrium are changed, the system tries to …… .

If the reaction is …… in one direction, it will be …… in the other.

		The equilibrium shifts to favour the...
……	**increases**	**...…… direction to take in heat energy.**
	decreases	**...exothermic direction to …… heat energy.**
Pressure	**increases**	**...side with …… moles of gas to …… the pressure.**
	decreases	**...side with …… moles of gas to …… the pressure.**

If …… of a …… is changed, the system will respond to …… .

If the concentration of...	**The system responds to...**
...……	**...make more products.**
...reactants ……	**...make more …… .**

Second Go: ..... /..... /.....

Reversible Reactions

Equilibrium

DYNAMIC EQUILIBRIUM —

Equilibrium can only be reached
....
....
....
....
....

If higher concentration

$$A + B \rightleftharpoons C + D$$

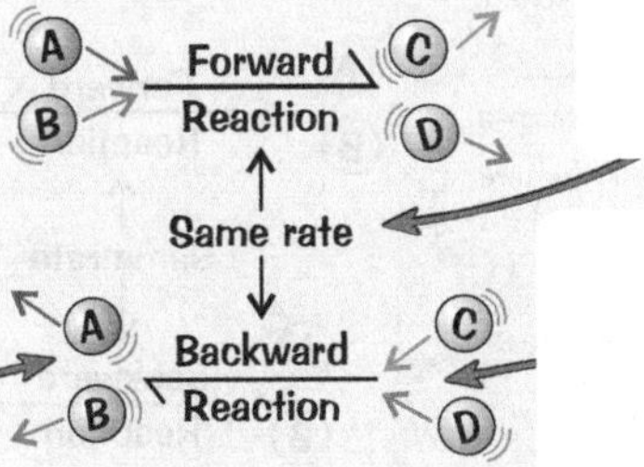

Haber Process

$$N_{2(g)} + 3H_{2(g)} \rightleftharpoons 2NH_{3(g)}$$

e.g.

Conditions:

-
-
-

Le Chatelier's Principle

If

are changed, the system tries to

.

If the reaction is
....
....
....
....

		The equilibrium shifts to favour the...
....	increases	... . direction to ....
	decreases	... . direction to ....
....	increases	...side with .... moles of gas ....
	decreases	...side with .... moles of gas ....

If concentration

If the concentration of...	The system responds to...
... .	...make ....
... .	...make ....

Mixed Practice Quizzes

Congratulations, you've made it through Topic 4. Now here are 4 sets of quiz questions covering p.67-74 to celebrate. You're very welcome.

Quiz 1 Date: / /

1) Name a metal that is found in the Earth's crust as an uncombined element. ☑

2) Is oxidation the gain or loss of electrons? ☑

3) What is meant by a dynamic equilibrium? ☑

4) How is a reactive metal such as potassium extracted from its ore? ☑

5) What is produced when a reactive metal reacts with water? ☑

6) What is a life cycle assessment? ☑

7) How will the position of equilibrium shift if the pressure
 of a reversible reaction between gases is lowered? ☑

8) True or false? Displacement reactions are redox reactions. ☑

9) What are the reactants in the Haber process? ☑

10) What is produced at the anode during the extraction of aluminium? ☑

Total: ☐

Quiz 2 Date: / /

1) Why isn't electrolysis always the method used to extract metals from ores? ☑

2) What is a redox reaction? ☑

3) True or false? The concentrations of reactants don't change at equilibrium. ☑

4) State whether the following list of metals is correctly ordered from
 most to least reactive — magnesium, sodium, aluminium, copper. ☑

5) What is carried out to evaluate the environmental impact of a new product? ☑

6) Describe how a metal's relative resistance to oxidation
 is related to its position in the reactivity series. ☑

7) State the temperature and pressure used in the Haber process. ☑

8) True or false? Unreactive metals readily form cations. ☑

9) Is it generally cheaper to recycle metals or to extract new metals? ☑

10) Give one benefit of using a biological method of metal extraction
 compared to traditional methods. ☑

Total: ☐

Mixed Practice Quizzes

Quiz 3 Date: / /

1) Give one way that recycling metals can be good for the environment. ☐

2) What can you say about the rates of the forward and backward reactions of a reversible reaction in a state of dynamic equilibrium? ☐

3) How is iron extracted from its ore? ☐

4) Give one way that a pure metal could be extracted from the metal compounds produced by phytoextraction or bioleaching. ☐

5) How would increasing the concentration of reactants affect a system at equilibrium? ☐

6) Is reduction the gain or loss of oxygen? ☐

7) True or false? Calcium will replace zinc in aqueous zinc sulfate. ☐

8) Where is the nitrogen used in the Haber process obtained from? ☐

9) Give a type of reaction you could carry out to determine whether one metal is more or less reactive than another metal. ☐

10) Which metal is more resistant to oxidation — magnesium or potassium? ☐

Total: ☐

Quiz 4 Date: / /

1) True or false? Equilibrium can only be reached in an open system. ☐

2) Give one example of a non-renewable resource. ☐

3) Name a metal that does not react with either dilute acid or water. ☐

4) What is used as the catalyst in the Haber process? ☐

5) In which direction will an equilibrium shift in response to an increase in temperature? ☐

6) Describe what occurs during a displacement reaction. ☐

7) If the equilibrium lies to the left, are there more reactants or products? ☐

8) Give the four stages of a product's life that are considered in a life cycle assessment. ☐

9) True or false? Calcium is less reactive than zinc. ☐

10) Outline how bacteria can be used to extract metals from their ores. ☐

Total: ☐

Metals and Alloys

First Go: ..... /..... /.....

Transition Metals

TRANSITION METALS — metals in the .

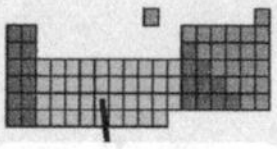

.... in the periodic table are transition metals.

Four typical properties of transition metals:

1. High
2. densities
3. Transition metals and their compounds can be — e.g. iron in the Haber process.
4. Their ions form compounds. e.g. Fe^{2+} Fe^{3+}

Alloys

ALLOY — a of a metal and at least .

Pure metals are as layers can each other.

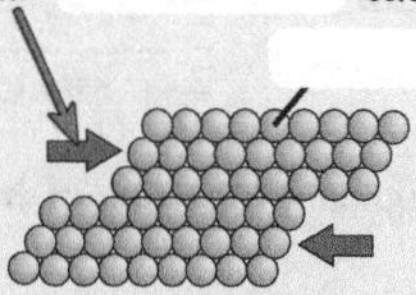

New element layers of metal atoms — they can't .

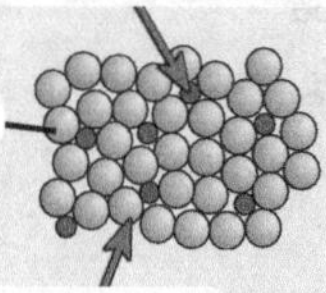

Alloys are than pure metals.

Uses of Metals and Alloys

Copper
Malleable and
— used in .
Good
— used for wiring.

Brass — alloy containing
.
— used for decorative taps, .

Steel — alloy containing
. added to make alloy steels.
to rust than iron — used to make things, e.g. .

Gold
Good
and corrosion resistant — used in components.
and
— used in jewellery.
Gold alloys also used for
— gold is
with e.g. zinc, copper, silver.

Aluminium is and
, but not very strong
— used in .
— alloy containing aluminium and about .
, lighter and more than aluminium
— used in cars, .

Second Go: ...../...../.....

Metals and Alloys

Transition Metals

TRANSITION METALS —

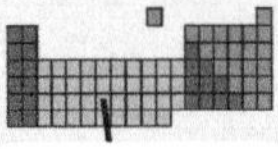

....
.... are transition metals.

Four typical properties of transition metals:

1.
2.
3. **Transition metals and their compounds can be**
   — e.g. iron in the .
4. **Their ions form** .
   e.g.

Alloys

ALLOY —

Pure metals as layers can .

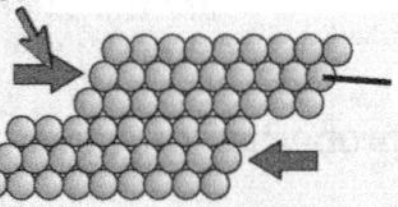

New element

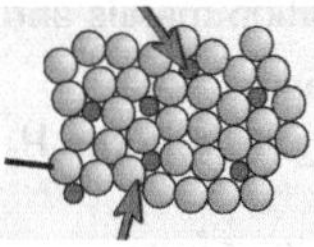

Alloys are

Uses of Metals and Alloys

Copper

Malleable

— used for wiring.

Brass —

Steel —

than iron — used to make .

Gold

Good **and**
— used in
.

Gold alloys also used for

Aluminium is

than aluminium
— used in .

Corrosion

First Go: ..... / ..... / .....

Corrosion and Rusting

CORROSION — _____ when they are _____ by oxygen and water from _____.

RUSTING — corrosion of iron by _____ (from the air).

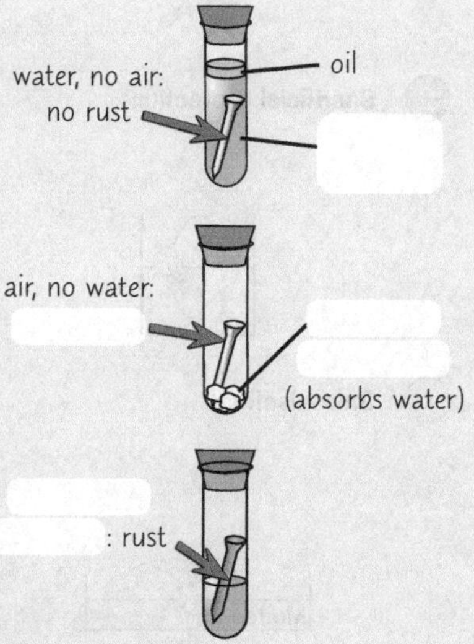

Three Ways to Prevent Rusting

1. **Barrier methods:** coating iron to keep out _____ _____, e.g. _____, oiling, greasing.

2. **Sacrificial protection:** attaching a _____ which corrodes _____.

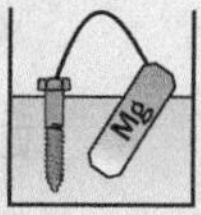

3. **Galvanisation:** _____ and _____. _____ is coated with a layer of more reactive _____.

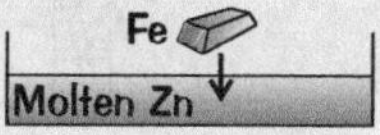

Electroplating

ELECTROPLATING — coating _____ with another metal using _____.

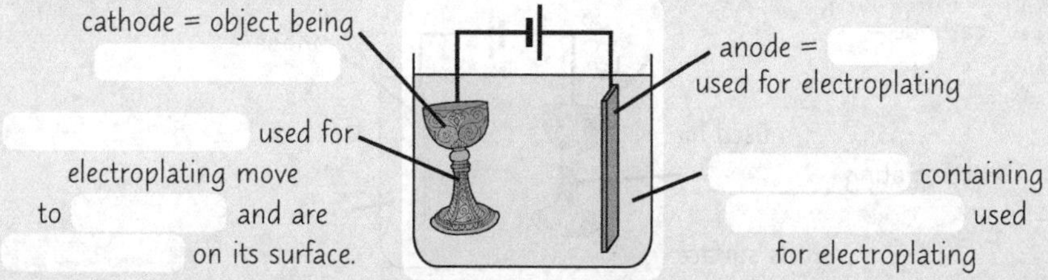

_____ can be coated onto items to prevent _____ — e.g. _____.

_____ can be coated onto items to improve _____ — e.g. _____.

Second Go:
..... /..... /.....

Corrosion

Corrosion and Rusting

CORROSION —

RUSTING —

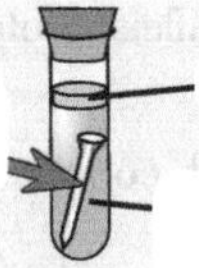

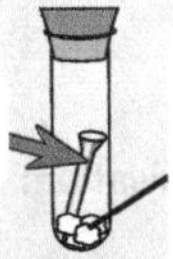

Three Ways to Prevent Rusting

1. **Barrier methods:**

2. **Sacrificial protection:**

3. **Galvanisation:**

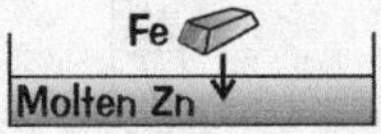

Electroplating

ELECTROPLATING —

cathode =

used for electroplating

on its surface.

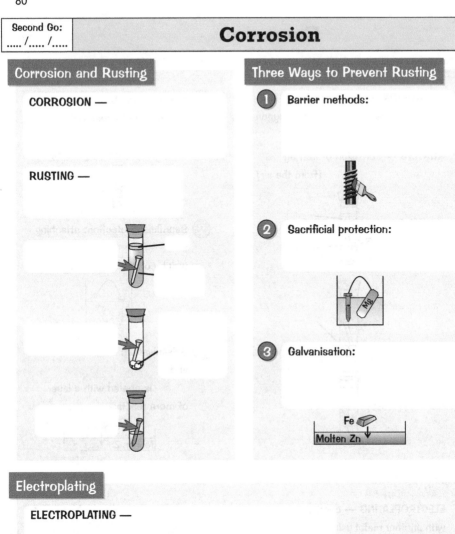

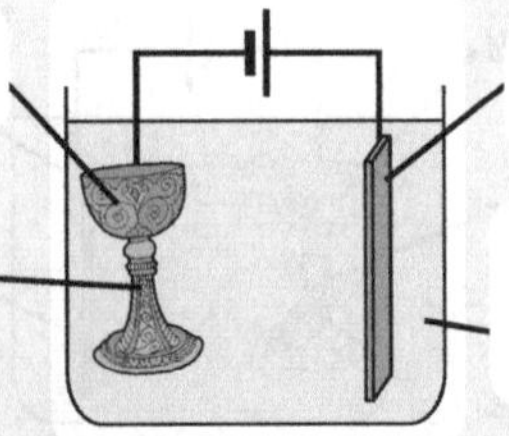

anode =

can be coated onto items .

can be coated onto items .

Gases and Titrations

First Go: ..... /..... /.....

Molar Volume

MOLAR VOLUME — volume occupied by ____.

molar volume = $\frac{\text{\_\_\_\_}}{\text{number of moles}}$

AVOGADRO'S LAW — under same ____, all gases have same ____.

At ____ ____ (RTP), molar volume of ____ = 24 dm^3 mol^{-1}.

RTP = ... and ....

Calculations With Gases

Use balanced equations and ____ ____ used up in a reaction to work out ____:

Use ____ of solid to work out number of moles ____.

↓

Use balanced equation to find ____.

↓

____ produced = moles of gas × ____.

Calculating Concentration from Titrations

Two ways to calculate concentration:

Concentration = ...	Units
____ of solute / ____ of solution	____ dm^{-3}
____ of solute / ____ of solution	____ dm^{-3}

(Units: ÷ M_r of solute converts between the two; ____)

TITRATION — method to find ____ of acid needed to ____ (or vice versa).

Use results of a titration to calculate ____:

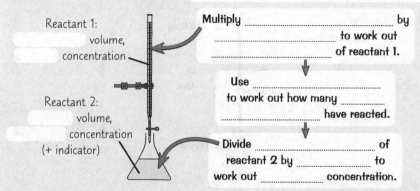

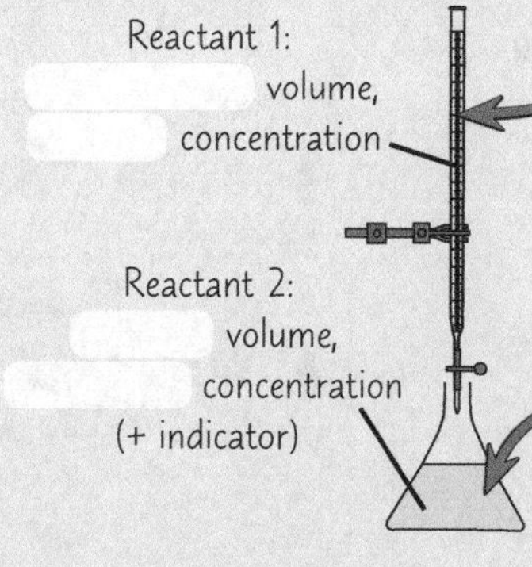

Multiply .... by .... to work out .... of reactant 1.

↓

Use .... to work out how many .... have reacted.

↓

Divide .... of reactant 2 by .... to work out .... concentration.

Second Go:
...../...../.....

Gases and Titrations

Molar Volume

MOLAR VOLUME —

=

AVOGADRO'S LAW —

= 24 dm^3 mol^{-1}.

RTP = ...

Calculations With Gases

Use balanced equations and

to

work out :

Use

to work out

.

Use balanced equation

Calculating Concentration from Titrations

Two ways to calculate concentration:

Concentration = ...	Units

TITRATION —

Use to calculate

:

Reactant 1:

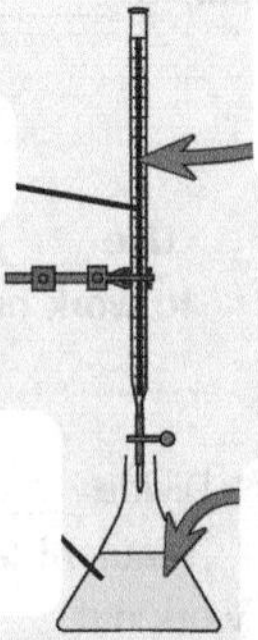

Reactant 2:

Multiply

Use

Divide

Mixed Practice Quizzes

Halfway through Topic 5 — I think it's about time for some quizzes and a nice cup of tea. Here are four quizzes to test you on p.77-82, anyway. (Tea not included, sorry...)

Quiz 1

Date: ...... / ...... / ......

1) Which set of metals make good catalysts?
2) Describe how to convert between units of g dm^{-3} and mol dm^{-3}.
3) Which two elements are in brass?
4) What two conditions are required for iron to rust?
5) True or false? To work out the volume of gas produced in a reaction from the mass of a reactant, you must know the balanced equation.
6) How does a sacrificial metal stop iron from rusting?
7) Name an alloy used to build bridges.
8) Give the equation used to find the molar volume of a gas.
9) Give two real-world applications of electroplating.
10) What happens to the layers of atoms in a metal when a new element is added to form an alloy?

Total:

Quiz 2

Date: ...... / ...... / ......

1) Which rust prevention method is both a barrier and a sacrificial method?
2) Describe the typical densities of transition metals.
3) True or false? One mole of any gas will occupy the same volume under the same conditions.
4) Why are metals malleable?
5) What properties of magnalium make it useful in the production of aircraft?
6) Give the equation to calculate concentration in units of mol dm^{-3}.
7) Give one property of transition metal ions.
8) What is corrosion?
9) What properties of copper make it suitable for making water pipes?
10) What type of ions should the electrolyte contain in electroplating?

Total:

Mixed Practice Quizzes

Quiz 3

Date: ...... / ...... / ......

1) What is meant by the term 'alloy'?
2) Give two methods of adding a protective barrier to a metal.
3) In electroplating, the metal being used to plate another object acts as which electrode?
4) Will iron rust if it is placed in a test tube containing only air?
5) Give one use of gold alloys.
6) Explain why an iron nail will not rust if it is placed in boiled water with a layer of oil sitting on top.
7) Describe the typical melting points of transition metals.
8) Why are alloys stronger than pure metals?
9) Explain how to use the results of a titration to find an unknown concentration of a solution of acid or alkali.
10) True or false? RTP = 20 °C and 1 atm.

Total:

Quiz 4

Date: ...... / ...... / ......

1) What term means 'the volume occupied by one mole of gas'?
2) True or false? Most metals in the periodic table are not transition metals.
3) What term is given to a substance that is a mixture of a metal and at least one other element?
4) Give two ways that the properties of steel differ from those of iron.
5) Describe how to work out the volume of a gas produced in a reaction when you know the mass of one of the solid reactants.
6) State 'Avogadro's law'.
7) True or false? When metals corrode, they are oxidised.
8) What is electroplating?
9) Name two elements which can be added to gold to produce gold alloys.
10) Give three ways to prevent iron from rusting.

Total:

Percentage Yield and Atom Economy

First Go: ...../...../.....

Percentage Yield

YIELD — the made in a reaction.

— how much product you get ( ) compared to how much you'd get converted to products ( ).

Percentage yield = × 100

% yield = waste of reactants + costs

Factors Affecting the Yield

Percentage yields are usually than %.

Three common reasons for this:

1. reaction — reactants converted.
2. losses — e.g. when transferring product .
3. — reactants don't make product.

Atom Economy

ATOM ECONOMY — of the molecular mass of reactants that gets .

Atom economy = × 100

Three advantages of using reactions with atom economies:

1. Use up at a rate.
2. a lot of waste.
3.

This means they are .

When choosing a reaction pathway, the ...., rate, ..., ..., atom economy and usefulness of .... are all considered.

Second Go: ...../...../.....

Percentage Yield and Atom Economy

Percentage Yield

YIELD — .

PERCENTAGE YIELD —

Percentage yield =

% yield =

Factors Affecting the Yield

Percentage yields are .

Three for this:

1

2 — e.g. when

.

3 — reactants don't make .

Atom Economy

ATOM ECONOMY —

Atom economy =

Three advantages

1

at a .

2

3

When choosing ....
....
....
....
....
....

The Haber Process

First Go: ...../...../.....

Producing Ammonia

reaction

$$\_\_\_ + 3H_{2(g)} \rightleftharpoons 2NH_{3(g)}$$

nitrogen hydrogen

Endothermic reaction

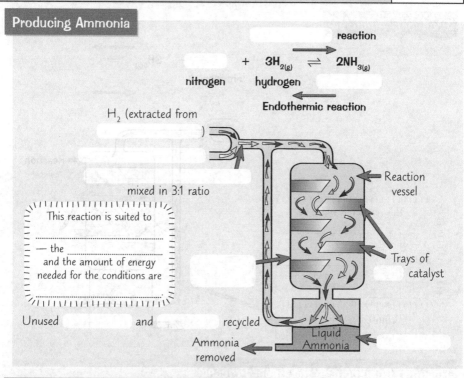

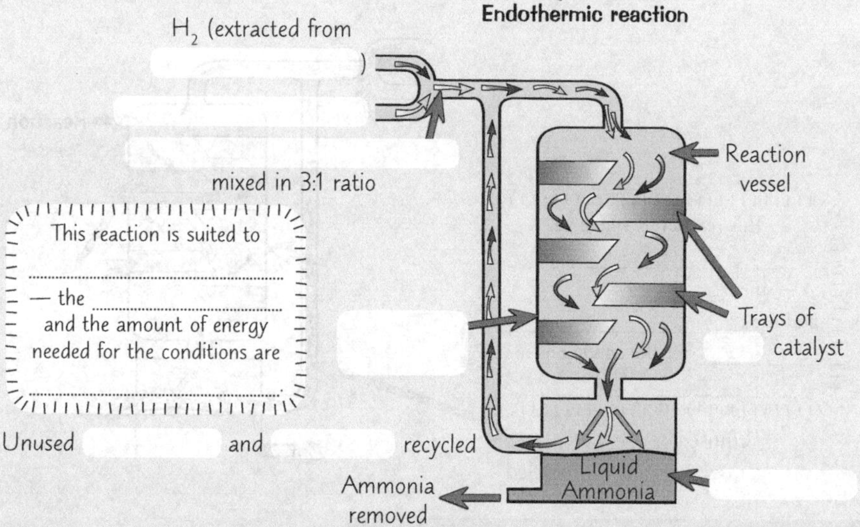

This reaction is suited to .... — the .... and the amount of energy needed for the conditions are ....

Reaction Conditions in the Haber Process

	Increase temperature		Increase reactant concentration	Use a
		Higher		
at which equilibrium reached	Faster		Faster	Faster

Reaction temperature of 450 °C is a compromise between and higher yield.

increases rate of reaction — this means a lower temperature can be used, .

Pressure is kept without becoming .

These four factors increase for any reversible reaction.

Other industrial processes often have to .... between ....

Second Go:
...../...../.....

The Haber Process

Producing Ammonia

+ $3H_{2(g)}$ ⇌

nitrogen

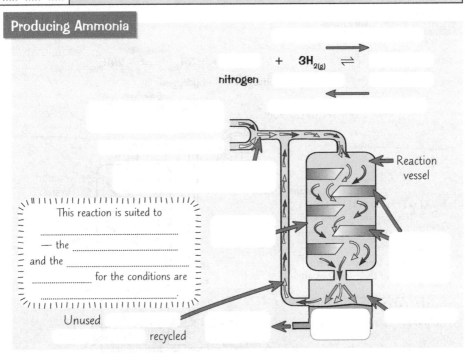

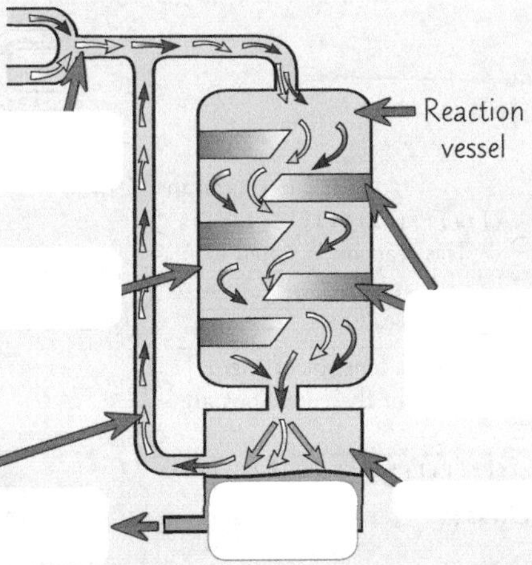

This reaction is suited to
....
— the ....
and the ....
.... for the conditions are
....

Unused

recycled

Reaction Conditions in the Haber Process

	temperature		Increase reactant	
		Higher		
				Faster

Reaction temperature of **is a**

.

rate of reaction

— this means

.

Pressure is kept

These four factors

Other industrial processes
....
....
....

Fertilisers and Fuel Cells

First Go: ..... / ..... / .....

Key Elements in Fertilisers

FERTILISERS — provide .... to plants to increase crop yields, by making them grow .... and ....

The main essential elements in fertilisers are .... and potassium.

Plants need these elements to ....

Ammonia Fertilisers

.... can be reacted with oxygen and water to produce ....

More ammonia can then be .... to make ammonium nitrate — a fertiliser:

$NH_{3(aq)} + HNO_{3(aq)} \rightarrow$ ....

Producing Ammonium Sulfate

.... is another ammonia fertiliser.

Laboratory production:

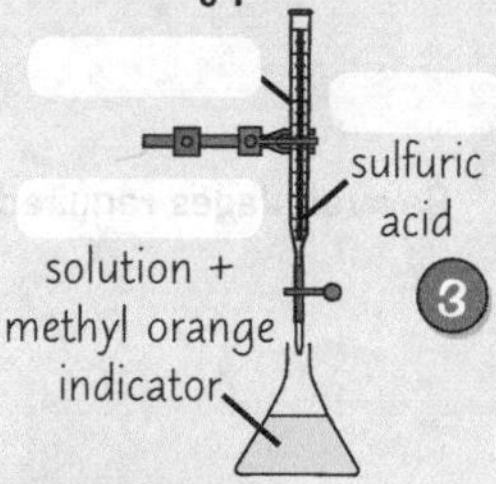

1. Do .... to work out exact ....
2. Mix reactants in ....
3. Form crystals by .... evaporating solution .... then leaving to cool.

Industrial production:

Not practical to use .... for large quantities.

Several stages required as .... made from .... first.

Fuel Cells

Chemical cells use a .... to produce a .... across the cell until ....

FUEL CELL — chemical cell that uses reaction of fuel and .... to produce ....

E.g. .... fuel cells produce a voltage. The only .... is water: .... $\rightarrow 2H_2O$.

Evaluating hydrogen-oxygen fuel cells:

Advantages	Disadvantages
Very .... — electricity generated .... so fewer places for	H_2 difficult to .... : • .... needed • explosive so must be ....
.... — don't produce .... or other pollutants.	H_2 has to be produced from either: • .... (non-renewable) • water (uses ....)

Second Go: ..... /..... /.....

Fertilisers and Fuel Cells

Key Elements in Fertilisers

FERTILISERS —

The main essential elements

Plants need

to .

Ammonia Fertilisers

can be reacted with

to produce .

can then be

to make

— a :

$NH_{3(aq)} + HNO_{3(aq)} \rightarrow$

Producing Ammonium Sulfate

.... is another ammonia fertiliser.

Laboratory production:

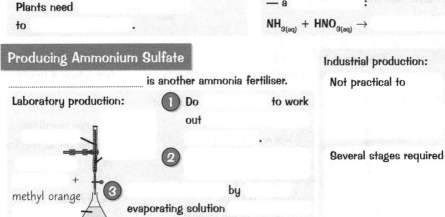

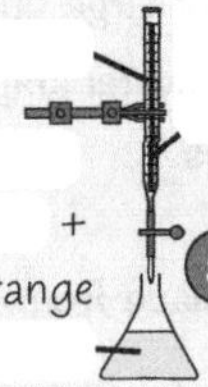

1. Do to work out .
2.
3. by evaporating solution then leaving to .

Industrial production:

Not practical to

Several stages required

Fuel Cells

Chemical cells use

E.g. .... produce .... The only ....: .... → $2H_2O$.

FUEL CELL — chemical cell that

Evaluating hydrogen-oxygen fuel cells:

Advantages	Disadvantages
.... — electricity	H_2 difficult to store: • • explosive so
	H_2 has to be produced from either: • •

Mixed Practice Quizzes

And that's the second half of Topic 5 done — fantastic! Now use these quizzes to test yourself on p.85-90 and work out your percentage yield at the end.

Quiz 1

Date: ...... / ...... / ......

1) Give a reason why a reaction's percentage yield may be lower than 100%.
2) Why is a low temperature not used in the Haber process even though it would maximise yield?
3) What is the purpose of a fertiliser?
4) Give two advantages of using reactions with higher atom economies.
5) Give one problem associated with the production of H_2 for fuel cells.
6) Give the equation for calculating percentage yield.
7) Name two ammonium salts that can act as fertilisers.
8) True or false? Increasing the percentage yield of a reaction results in less waste and lower costs.
9) How does a chemical cell work?
10) How does increasing the temperature of a reversible reaction affect the rate at which the equilibrium is reached?

Total:

Quiz 2

Date: ...... / ...... / ......

1) Give a definition of the term 'atom economy'.
2) What is the difference between 'yield' and 'percentage yield'?
3) How do higher temperatures affect the yield of the Haber process?
4) What two reactants can be used to make ammonium sulfate?
5) What is the waste product of the reaction in a hydrogen-oxygen fuel cell?
6) True or false? Percentage yields are usually lower than 100%.
7) Give four ways that the rate at which equilibrium is reached in a reversible reaction could be increased.
8) Give the equation for the reaction between ammonia and nitric acid.
9) Does a higher atom economy make a reaction more or less sustainable?
10) Why is an extremely high pressure not used in the Haber process?

Total:

Mixed Practice Quizzes

Quiz 3

Date: ...... / ...... / ......

1) What is a fuel cell?
2) Give an equation used to calculate the atom economy of a reaction.
3) Give one problem associated with the storage of H_2 gas for use in fuel cells.
4) What happens to unreacted hydrogen and nitrogen in the Haber process?
5) How would a reduction in percentage yield affect the cost of a reaction?
6) Give an example of how practical losses can reduce percentage yield.
7) Why is the laboratory method for ammonium sulfate preparation not also used in industry?
8) How does increasing the pressure affect the yield of the Haber process?
9) Name three essential elements in fertilisers.
10) Give two other factors that are considered when choosing a reaction pathway for industry, as well as atom economy and percentage yield.

Total:

Quiz 4

Date: ...... / ...... / ......

1) Define 'yield' in terms of chemical reactions.
2) Why are hydrogen and nitrogen suitable raw materials for producing ammonia on an industrial scale?
3) Is the forward reaction in the Haber process exothermic or endothermic?
4) Give two advantages of using hydrogen-oxygen fuel cells.
5) Why does the industrial production of ammonium sulfate involve several stages?
6) Describe how you could prepare ammonium sulfate crystals in the lab.
7) What are the reactants in a hydrogen-oxygen fuel cell?
8) What allows a lower temperature to be used in the Haber process without reducing the rate of reaction?
9) Why would unwanted reactions reduce the percentage yield of a reaction?
10) True or false? Reactions with high atom economies produce lots of waste.

Total:

Group 1 and Group 0 Elements

First Go: ..... /..... /.....

Alkali Metals

.... — common name for ....

Group 1 elements all have .... in their ....

7 3 Li
23 11 Na
39 19 K
85 37 Rb
133 55 Cs
223 87 Fr

Properties of Group 1 Metals

Group 1 metals have .... properties from most other metals:

They're much ....

They're ....

They have .... melting and ....

Reactivity of Group 1 Elements

Readily lose .... outer electron to form ....

.... down Group 1 as outer electron is .... from nucleus and .... lost.

Alkali metals .... with water to make .... :

.... metal + ... → metal hydroxide + hydrogen

e.g. sodium + ... → .... + hydrogen

Use the trend down Group 1 to predict ....

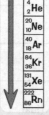

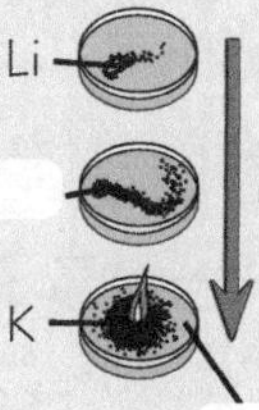

DOWN Group 1: more ...., movement, and ....

Group 0 Elements

These elements are also known as ....

GROUP 0 ELEMENTS — non-metals with ....

.... are very stable, so these elements are ....

All Group 0 elements are .... at room temperature.

As you go .... Group 0:	
....	increases
Melting and boiling points	....

4 2 He
20 10 Ne
40 18 Ar
84 36 Kr
131 54 Xe
222 86 Rn

Property	Uses
....	.... during welding
Non-flammable	........, flash photography
.... (just helium)	.... balloons, airships

Second Go: ...../...../.....

Group 1 and Group 0 Elements

Alkali Metals

Li
$^{7}_{3}$Li
$^{23}_{11}$Na
$^{39}_{19}$K
$^{85}_{37}$Rb
$^{133}_{55}$Cs
$^{223}_{87}$Fr

Group 1 elements all

Properties of Group 1 Metals

Group 1 metals have

They're .

They have

Reactivity of Group 1 Elements

Use the trend .... Group 1 to predict ....

....

Readily lose

down Group 1 as

.

Alkali metals

DOWN Group 1:

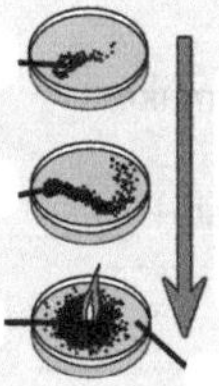

.... + ... → .... + ...

....

e.g. sodium + ... → .... + ...

....

Group 0 Elements

These elements ....

GROUP 0 ELEMENTS — .

All Group 0 elements are

As you go	
points	

$^{4}_{2}$He
$^{20}_{10}$Ne
$^{40}_{18}$Ar
$^{84}_{36}$Kr
$^{131}_{54}$Xe
$^{222}_{86}$Rn

Property	Uses
(just)	

Group 7 Elements

First Go: ..... / ..... / .....

Halogens

HALOGENS — the non-metal elements in .

The halogens exist as .... — two atoms joined by a .... bond.

Halogen	Appearance at room temperature
Chlorine	gas
Bromine	red-brown which gives off
	which gives off purple vapour

Chlorine gas turns white.

at room temperature show melting and boiling points .

19/9	F
35.5/17	Cl
80/35	Br
127/53	I
210/85	At

Reactions of Group 7 Elements

Halogens have — they gain one electron to form .

down Group 7 as outer shell is from nucleus so it's harder to .

Hydrogen halides form .... (e.g. hydrochloric acid) when ....

.... + halogen → metal halide

e.g. sodium + chlorine → ....

.... + halogen → hydrogen halide

e.g. .... + chlorine → ....

Halogen Displacement Reactions

Displacement reactions are .... reactions.

Start with →	$KCl_{(aq)}$ (colourless)	$KBr_{(aq)}$ ( )	$KI_{(aq)}$ (colourless)
add (colourless) →	no reaction	orange solution ( )	brown solution ( )
add $Br_{2(aq)}$ ( ) →			solution (I_2)
add ( ) →		no reaction	

Chlorine displaces bromine from .

$Cl_{2(aq)} + 2KBr_{(aq)} \rightarrow$ .... + ...

chlorine gains electrons (..................) — bromide ions lose electrons (..................)

Results of displacement reactions show ....

You'd predict .... wouldn't displace other halogens as it's at the .... of Group 7.

Second Go:	
...... /...... /......	

Group 7 Elements

Halogens

HALOGENS —

⌇⌇⌇⌇⌇⌇⌇⌇⌇⌇⌇⌇⌇⌇⌇⌇⌇⌇⌇⌇⌇⌇⌇⌇⌇⌇⌇⌇⌇⌇
The halogens exist as
...
...
⌇⌇⌇⌇⌇⌇⌇⌇⌇⌇⌇⌇⌇⌇⌇⌇⌇⌇⌇⌇⌇⌇⌇⌇⌇⌇⌇⌇⌇⌇

Halogen	Appearance at room temperature
Bromine	red-brown

← Chlorine gas

← show melting and boiling points

$^{19}_{9}$F	
$^{35.5}_{17}$Cl	
$^{80}_{35}$Br	
$^{127}_{53}$I	
$^{210}_{85}$At	

Reactions of Group 7 Elements

Halogens have

⌇⌇⌇⌇⌇⌇⌇⌇⌇⌇⌇⌇⌇⌇⌇⌇⌇⌇⌇⌇⌇⌇⌇⌇⌇⌇
Hydrogen halides form
...
...
...
⌇⌇⌇⌇⌇⌇⌇⌇⌇⌇⌇⌇⌇⌇⌇⌇⌇⌇⌇⌇⌇⌇⌇⌇

down Group 7 as

.... + →

.... + →

e.g. sodium + chlorine → e.g. + chlorine →

Halogen Displacement Reactions

Start with ➡	KCl$_{(aq)}$ (colourless)	KBr$_{(aq)}$	
(colourless) ➡	no reaction	orange solution	brown solution
add ➡			
add ➡			

Chlorine

from

$Cl_{2(aq)}$ + → +

.... bromide ions lose
.... electrons (....................)

⌇⌇⌇⌇⌇⌇⌇⌇⌇⌇⌇⌇⌇⌇⌇⌇⌇⌇⌇⌇⌇⌇⌇⌇⌇⌇
Results of displacement
reactions show
...
You'd predict
.... as it's
at the
⌇⌇⌇⌇⌇⌇⌇⌇⌇⌇⌇⌇⌇⌇⌇⌇⌇⌇⌇⌇⌇⌇⌇⌇⌇⌇

☹ ☑ 🙂 ☑ 😊 ☑

Mixed Practice Quizzes

Now you've had a look at three groups of the periodic table on p.93-96, here are four groups of quiz questions about them. See what I did there?

Quiz 1

Date: ...... / ...... / ......

1) How does reactivity change as you go down Group 1?
2) True or false? Group 0 elements generally exist as molecules.
3) What is another name for the Group 7 elements?
4) How many outer shell electrons do Group 1 elements have?
5) True or false? Bromine can displace chlorine from an aqueous solution of its salt.
6) How does reactivity change as you go down Group 7?
7) Give a word equation for the reaction of sodium with water.
8) Describe the appearance of bromine at room temperature.
9) When chlorine displaces another Group 7 element from its compound, is it oxidised or reduced?
10) Give a possible use for an inert gas with a low density.

Total:

Quiz 2

Date: ...... / ...... / ......

1) What type of solution is formed when hydrogen halides dissolve in water?
2) Describe how your observations would differ between the reaction of lithium with water and the reaction of potassium with water.
3) What colour is chlorine gas?
4) True or false? Group 1 metals form alkalis when they react with water.
5) How does the electronic structure of a halogen change when it reacts?
6) What are the Group 0 elements also known as?
7) What state do the Group 0 elements exist in at room temperature?
8) Describe a test you could perform to see if a gas is chlorine.
9) Give two ways that the properties of Group 1 metals differ from other metals.
10) Why are the Group 0 elements unreactive?

Total:

Mixed Practice Quizzes

Quiz 3

Date: ...... / ...... / ......

1) What type of compound is formed when a metal reacts with a halogen?
2) True or false? Group 1 metals are softer than most other metals.
3) How many atoms make up a halogen molecule?
4) What happens to the boiling points of the Group 0 elements as you go down the group?
5) What is an alternative name for the Group 1 metals?
6) Which halogen is a dark grey solid at room temperature?
7) Describe the electronic structure of the Group 0 elements.
8) True or false? Halogen displacement reactions are redox reactions.
9) How does the electronic structure of Group 1 metals change when they react?
10) What would you observe when bromine (Br_2) water is added to a solution of potassium iodide (KI)?

Total:

Quiz 4

Date: ...... / ...... / ......

1) True or false? Group 0 elements are flammable gases.
2) How do the melting points of Group 1 metals compare to the melting points of other metals?
3) How many electrons are in the outer shell of a halogen atom?
4) What is produced when a Group 1 metal reacts with water?
5) What is the product of the reaction between chlorine and hydrogen?
6) How do the boiling points of halogens change as you move down Group 7?
7) Why do Group 1 metals get more reactive as you move down the group?
8) Explain why the reactivity of Group 7 elements decreases as you move down the group.
9) Why are some noble gases used in filament lamps?
10) What happens when a more reactive halogen reacts with a compound of a less reactive halogen in solution?

Total:

Rates of Reaction

First Go: ..... / ..... / .....

Measuring Rates of Reaction

RATE OF REACTION — how .... happens.

Rate of reaction = $\frac{\dots\dots}{\text{Time}}$ or $\frac{\dots\dots}{\text{Time}}$

Units of rate depend on .... — they're in the form ....

Three common ....: g s^{-1}, ..., mol dm^{-3} s^{-1}

Three ways to measure rate of reaction:

1. time to form a ....
2. change in .... over time
3. .... produced over time

Comparing Rates of Reaction

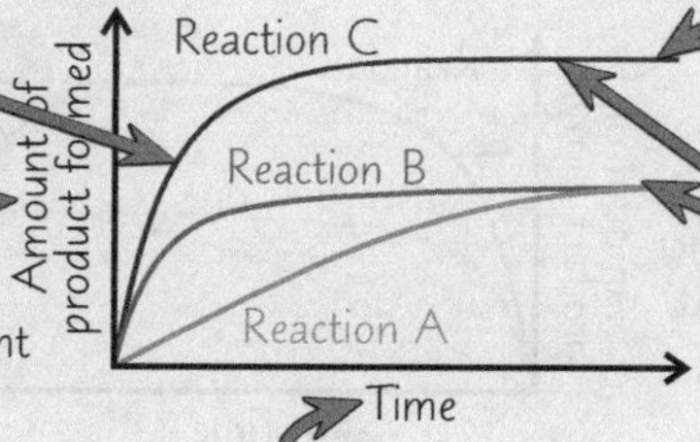

.... show a .... rate of reaction.

Amount of .... can be measured in different ways: e.g. .... (g), ... (cm^3) or concentration (mol dm^{-3}).

.... can be formed by using ....

.... the reaction ....

Time is normally ....

Calculating Rates from Graphs

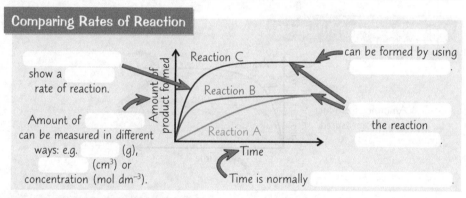

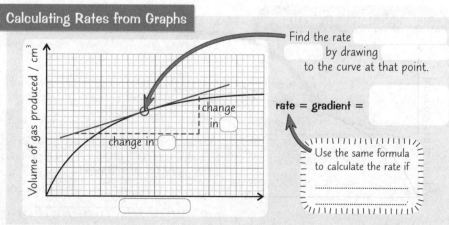

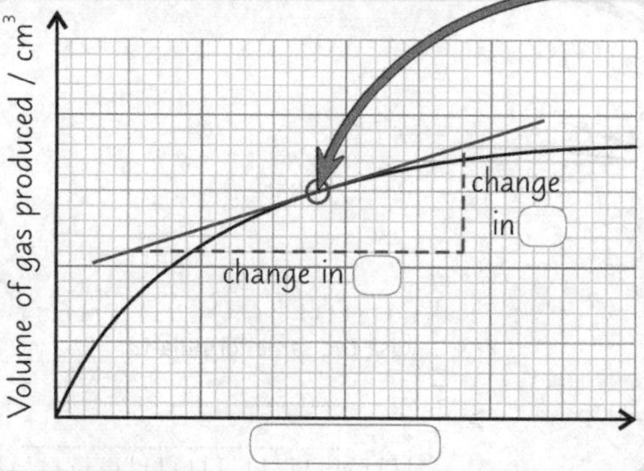

Find the rate .... by drawing .... to the curve at that point.

rate = gradient = ...

Use the same formula to calculate the rate if ....

Second Go: ...../...../.....

Rates of Reaction

Measuring Rates of Reaction

RATE OF REACTION — .

Rate of reaction = ... or ....

Units of rate

.... :

....

Three ways to measure rate of reaction:

Comparing Rates of Reaction

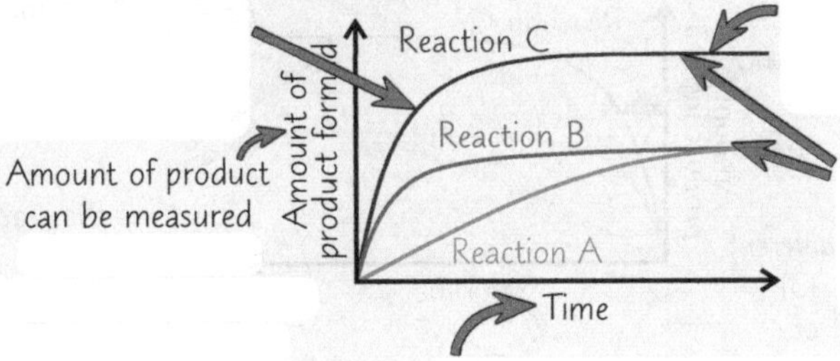

Calculating Rates from Graphs

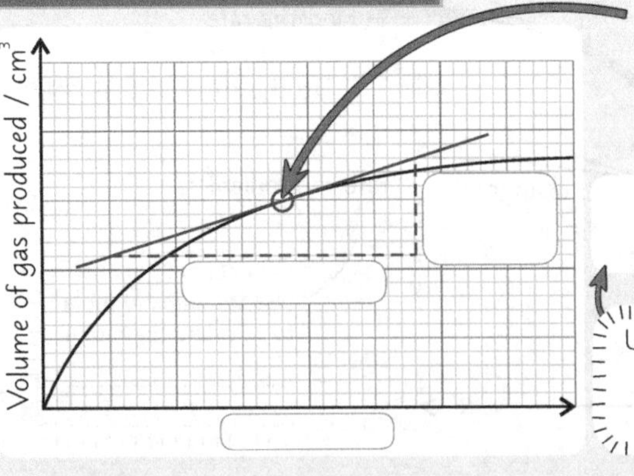

Use the same formula to ....

....

....

Factors Affecting Rates of Reaction

First Go: ..... /..... /.....

Collision Theory

Reactions happen if particles collide with ....

ACTIVATION ENERGY — minimum amount of ...... that ....

Rate depends on...

Collision frequency — the ...... between particles, the ...... the rate of reaction.

Collision energy — the more collisions with ...... , the ...... the rate of reaction.

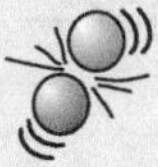

High
High
Fast

Low
Low
Slow

Temperature

Particles ...... and collide more ...... with more energy.

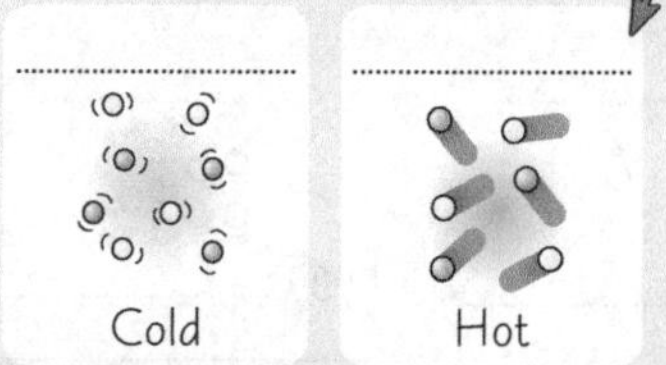

Pressure or Concentration

...... in the same ...... — more frequent ....

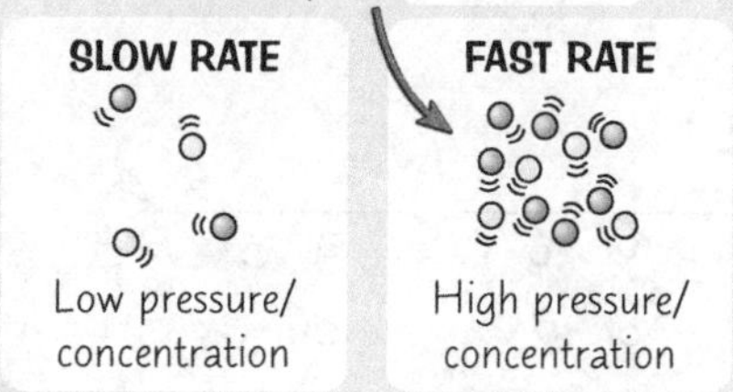

Surface Area

...... for particles to ...... with — more ...... collisions.

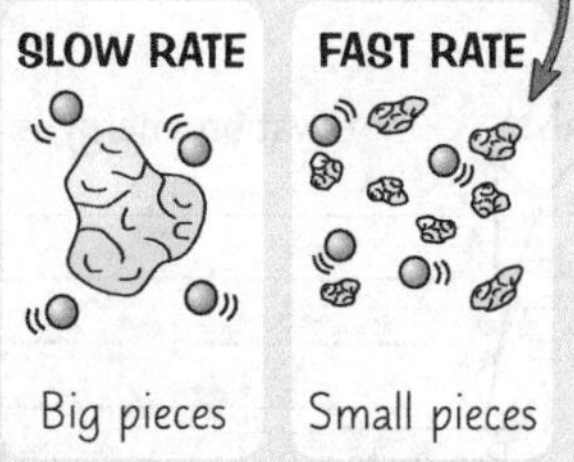

The .... the piece of solid, the larger the .... ratio.

Catalysts

CATALYST — ...... reaction without being ...... in the reaction, and without ....

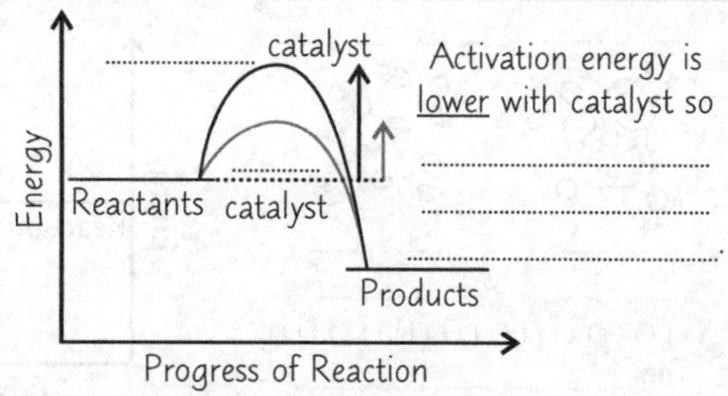

Activation energy is lower with catalyst so ....

Enzymes are ....
They can be used to make ....

Second Go: ...../...../.....

Factors Affecting Rates of Reaction

Collision Theory

Reactions happen if .

ACTIVATION ENERGY —

Rate depends on...

Collision frequency —

Collision energy —

Temperature

....

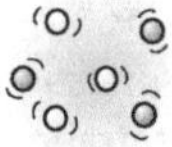

....

....

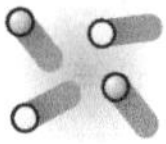

....

Pressure or Concentration

....

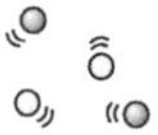

Low ..../

....

....

High ..../

....

Surface Area

....

....

....

....

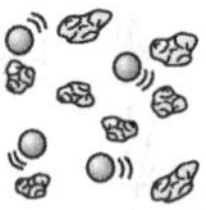

....

....

The ....

.............., the ....

....

....

Catalysts

CATALYST —

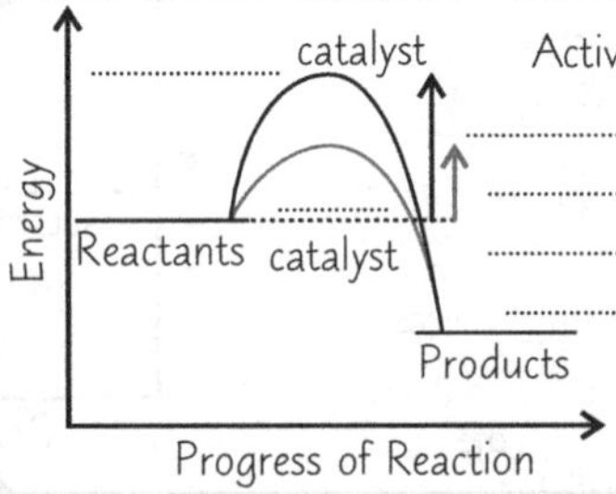

Activation energy is ....

....

....

....

Enzymes are ....

They can be ....

Endothermic & Exothermic Reactions

First Go: ..... /..... /.....

Energy Transfer

ENDOTHERMIC REACTION — heat energy from the surroundings (shown by a in temperature).

EXOTHERMIC REACTION — heat energy to the surroundings (shown by a in temperature).

Measuring Temperature Change

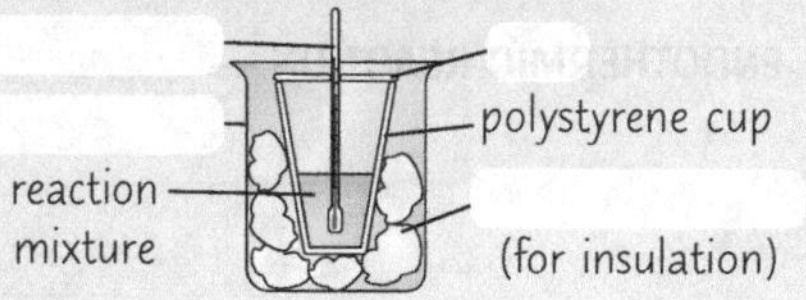

Record and **maximum/minimum** , **then calculate** .

You can use this method to investigate:

- in water
- **neutralisation,** and reactions.

Reaction Profiles

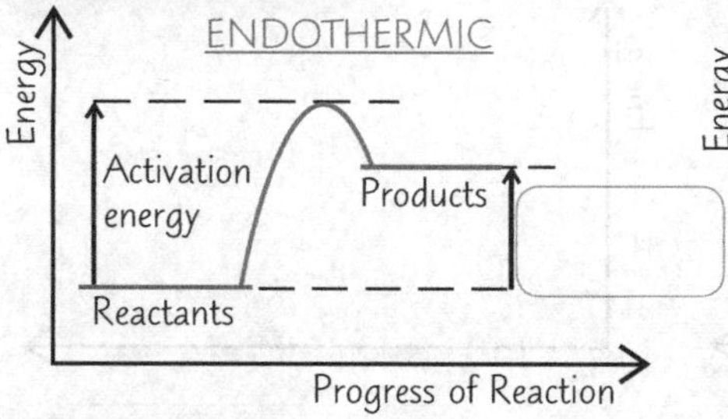

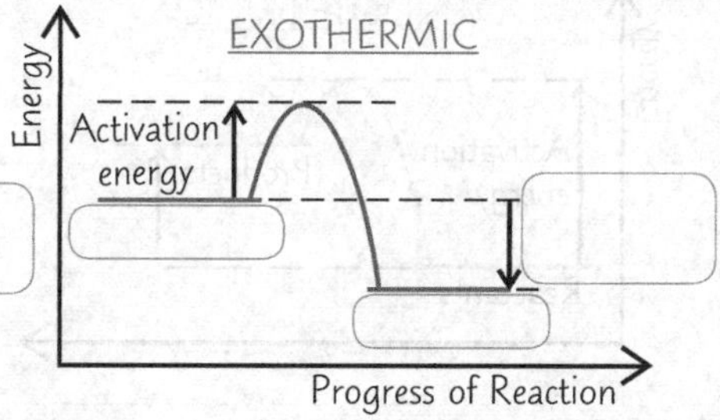

Bond Energies

BOND — ENDOTHERMIC

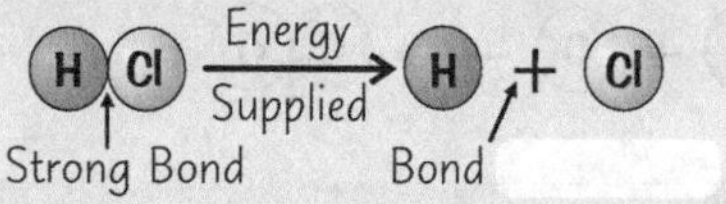

Endothermic reactions: energy used to than energy released by .

BOND — EXOTHERMIC

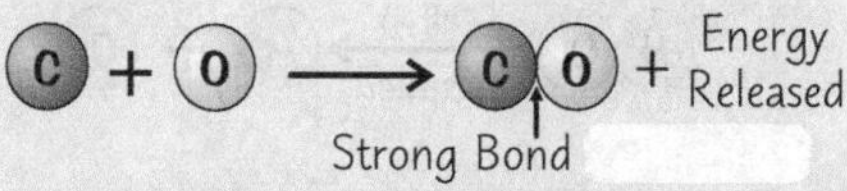

Exothermic reactions: energy released by than energy used to .

overall energy change = ... energy needed to .... − .... energy released by ....

These energies can be calculated from .

Second Go: ...../...../.....

Endothermic & Exothermic Reactions

Energy Transfer

ENDOTHERMIC REACTION —

EXOTHERMIC REACTION —

Measuring Temperature Change

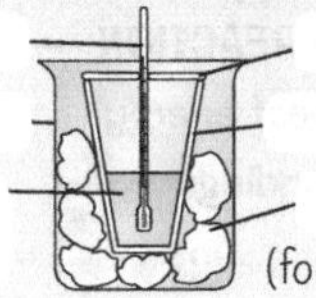

(for)

Record

You can use this method to investigate:

-
- .

Reaction Profiles

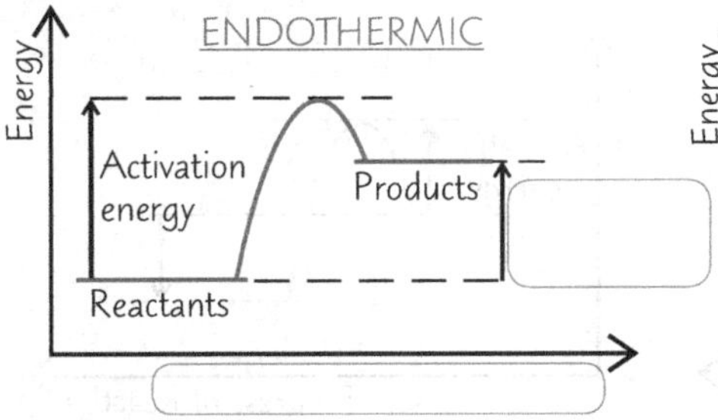
ENDOTHERMIC
Energy
Activation energy
Products
Reactants

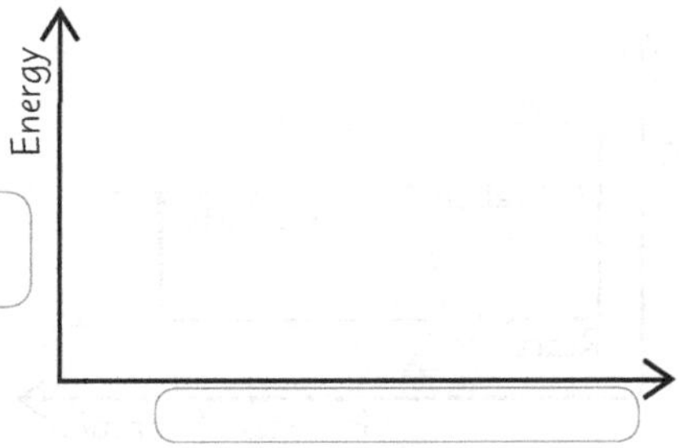
Energy

Bond Energies

— ENDOTHERMIC

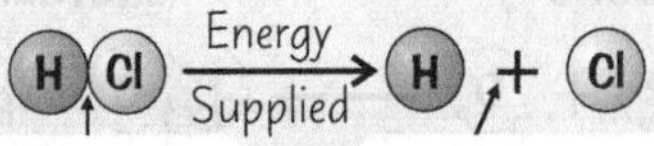

Endothermic reactions: energy used to

Exothermic reactions: energy released by

= – These energies

Mixed Practice Quizzes

Time to increase your rate of revision by throwing in a quiz catalyst. All of these questions are based on p.99-104, so make sure you've gone over those first.

Quiz 1

Date: ...... / ...... / ......

1) What type of reaction takes in heat energy from the surroundings?
2) Why does increasing the temperature of a reaction increase the rate?
3) True or false? Forming new bonds is an endothermic process.
4) What are biological catalysts called?
5) True or false? The rate of a reaction might have the units g cm^{-3}.
6) How is the energy released by an exothermic reaction shown on a reaction profile?
7) List the apparatus used to measure the temperature change of a reaction.
8) How does a catalyst affect the activation energy of a reaction?
9) True or false? The steeper the line on a rate graph, the faster the reaction.
10) How would you find the rate at a specific point on a rate graph?

Total:

Quiz 2

Date: ...... / ...... / ......

1) In the reaction profile for an endothermic reaction, are the reactants or products at higher energy?
2) What is represented by the horizontal axis on a rate graph?
3) Why does a higher pressure mean a faster rate of reaction between gases?
4) Give the equation for calculating rate of reaction from the amount of product formed and the time taken.
5) What's the minimum amount of energy that reactants need to react called?
6) True or false? In exothermic reactions, more energy is released by forming bonds than is used to break bonds.
7) Give one way of increasing the collision frequency of particles in a reaction.
8) Why might cotton wool be used when measuring temperature change?
9) Using collision theory, which two factors determine the rate of a reaction?
10) Give a formula for calculating the overall energy change of a reaction.

Total:

Mixed Practice Quizzes

Quiz 3

Date: ...... / ...... / ......

1) What type of reaction requires more energy to break bonds than is released in forming new ones?
2) What is the activation energy of a reaction?
3) How does increasing the concentration of the particles in a reaction affect the collision frequency?
4) Give two types of reaction suitable for a temperature change investigation.
5) How can you tell which reaction shown on a single graph has the fastest rate?
6) Give three things you could measure in a reaction to determine its rate.
7) Why does increasing the surface area of a reactant increase reaction rate?
8) Would you observe an increase or a decrease in the temperature of the surroundings in an exothermic reaction?
9) What is a catalyst?
10) True or false? Increasing collision frequency increases rate of reaction.

Total:

Quiz 4

Date: ...... / ...... / ......

1) What is represented on the horizontal axis of a reaction profile?
2) In which type of reaction does the temperature of the surroundings fall?
3) How can you tell from a rate graph when a reaction is finished?
4) True or false? In an exothermic reaction profile, the products are at a lower energy than the reactants.
5) How does decreasing the concentration of reactants in solution affect the rate of reaction?
6) What can the total energy needed to break bonds and the total energy released by forming bonds in a reaction be calculated from?
7) What is the formula used to calculate the rate of reaction from a graph?
8) Give one thing that enzymes can be used to make.
9) Which factor affects both collision frequency and collision energy?
10) True or false? A catalyst is used up in a reaction.

Total:

Hydrocarbons

First Go: ..... / ..... / .....

Crude Oil

CRUDE OIL — a complex mixture of

(mostly).

It's a resource.

.... only contain hydrogen and carbon atoms.

Used as to create useful substances in .

The have carbon atoms arranged in .

Properties of Hydrocarbons

The longer the hydrocarbon chain, the the — this affects properties.

As length of chain increases...
...boiling point ....
.... increases.
...ease of ignition ....

Hydrocarbons with longer chains contain more .... atoms. Each crude oil fraction contains hydrocarbons with ....

Combustion

COMPLETE COMBUSTION — a reaction that occurs when .

hydrocarbon + ... → .... + ...

Hydrocarbons are used as because combustion a lot of energy.

Homologous Series

HOMOLOGOUS SERIES — a family of which have the same and share .

.... are an example of a homologous series.

In a homologous series:

Molecular formulas of compounds differ by .

Physical properties with of molecule.

Second Go: ..... /..... /.....

Hydrocarbons

Crude Oil

CRUDE OIL —

Hydrocarbons only ....

Used as

Properties of Hydrocarbons

The longer the hydrocarbon chain, the

—

.

As length of chain ...

Hydrocarbons with longer chains .... Each crude oil fraction ....

Combustion

COMPLETE COMBUSTION —

.... + ... → .... + ...

Hydrocarbons are used as

Homologous Series

HOMOLOGOUS SERIES —

.... are an example of ....

In a homologous series:

Fractional Distillation and Cracking

First Go: ..... / ..... / .....

Fractional Distillation

FRACTIONAL DISTILLATION — a process used to ______ the ______ in crude oil into ______ according to ______.
Each fraction has different uses.

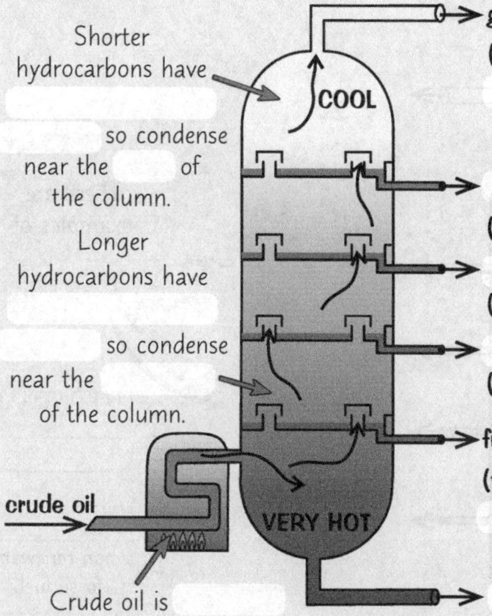

Methane (from ....) is also a non-renewable ....

Cracking

There is a ______ for fuels with ______ carbon chains.

Alkenes are used to make .... (mostly ....).

CRACKING — breaks down ______ hydrocarbons (alkanes) into ______ molecules.

______-chain alkane → ______ + ______ alkene

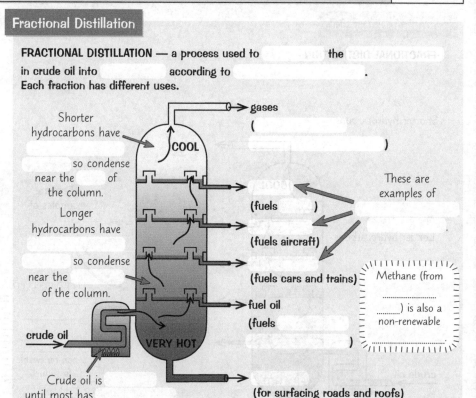

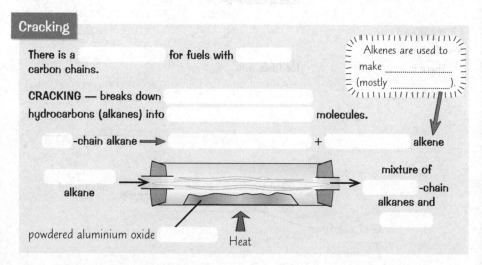

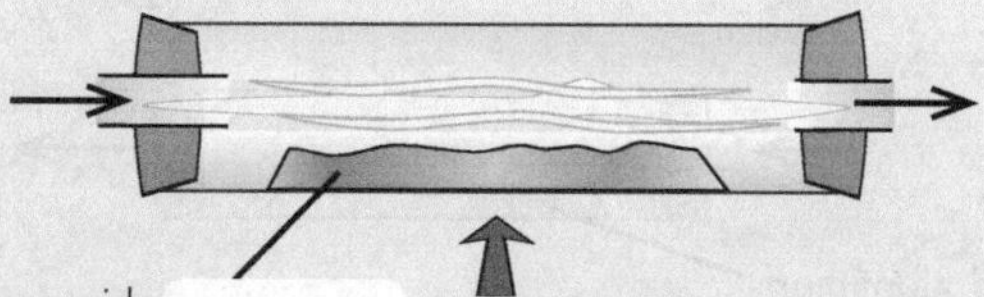

Second Go: ...../...../.....

Fractional Distillation and Cracking

Fractional Distillation

FRACTIONAL DISTILLATION —

Shorter hydrocarbons

Longer hydrocarbons

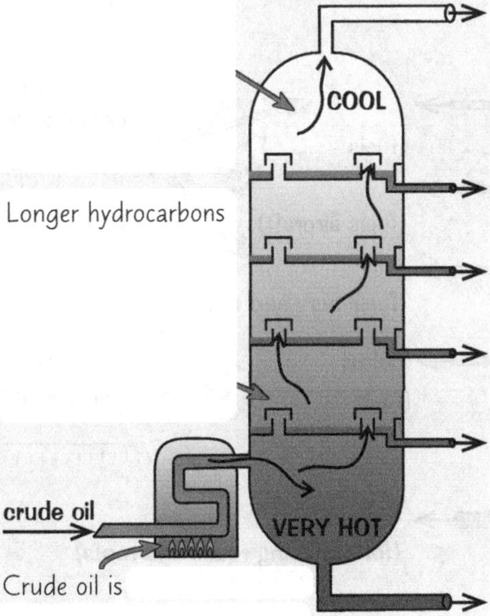

Crude oil is .

These are examples of .

....
....
....
.... a non-renewable fossil fuel.

Cracking

There is **for fuels with** .

CRACKING —

Alkenes are used ....
....
....

→ +

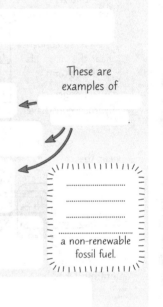

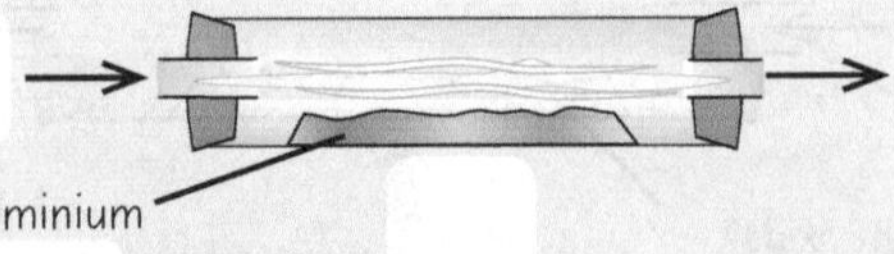

mixture of

Mixed Practice Quizzes

Hopefully you've cracked all the information on p.107-110, because it's time for some questions. Remember to check how well you've done afterwards.

Quiz 1 Date: / /

1) What type of molecule makes up crude oil? ☑

2) What is crude oil used for in the petrochemical industry? ☑

3) What is a homologous series? ☑

4) What is kerosene used for? ☑

5) Why are hydrocarbons used as fuels? ☑

6) What is the purpose of cracking hydrocarbons? ☑

7) Which fraction condenses nearer the bottom of the column during fractional distillation — fuel oil or petrol? ☑

8) What is the first thing that happens to crude oil during fractional distillation? ☑

9) When a hydrocarbon undergoes combustion, what does it react with? ☑

10) True or false? Crude oil is a renewable resource. ☑

Total: ☐

Quiz 2 Date: / /

1) True or false? The physical properties of compounds in a homologous series vary gradually with the length of molecule. ☑

2) Which two elements make up hydrocarbons? ☑

3) How are carbon atoms arranged in the hydrocarbon molecules in crude oil? ☑

4) True or false? When an alkane is cracked, only alkenes are produced. ☑

5) Which fraction of crude oil is used for domestic heating and cooking? ☑

6) Give an example of a homologous series. ☑

7) How is the length of a hydrocarbon chain related to viscosity? ☑

8) What are the products of complete combustion of a hydrocarbon fuel? ☑

9) Name three fuels produced from the fractional distillation of crude oil. ☑

10) Where do shorter hydrocarbons condense in a fractionating column? ☑

Total: ☐

Mixed Practice Quizzes

Quiz 3

Date: ...... / ...... / ......

1) Are long-chain hydrocarbons easier to ignite than short-chain hydrocarbons?
2) True or false? Cracking produces larger hydrocarbons from shorter ones.
3) What is fractional distillation?
4) Are alkenes saturated or unsaturated?
5) Which fraction of crude oil is used as a fuel for ships?
6) How does the chain length of a hydrocarbon affect its boiling point?
7) Natural gas contains which fossil fuel?
8) What is the name for a family of molecules with the same general formula and similar chemical properties?
9) What type of hydrocarbon is crude oil mostly made of?
10) What is complete combustion?

Total:

Quiz 4

Date: ...... / ...... / ......

1) What is cracking?
2) Give three examples of non-renewable fossil fuels.
3) What type of compound contains carbon and hydrogen atoms only?
4) True or false? Alkanes are an example of a homologous series.
5) What is bitumen used for?
6) Are alkanes saturated or unsaturated?
7) What is the word equation for the complete combustion of a hydrocarbon?
8) How do the molecular formulas of neighbouring compounds in a homologous series differ?
9) True or false? Each crude oil fraction contains hydrocarbons with a similar number of carbon atoms.
10) True or false? Fractionating columns are hotter at the top than the bottom.

Total:

Pollutants and Fuels

First Go: ...../...../.....

Air Pollution

Fossil fuels contain __________ and sometimes __________.

__________ releases __________ which pollute the air. ← This can happen in appliances that are ....

Pollutant	Formation	Effects
....	.... 	Stops blood from transporting .... around the body — this can cause ...., ... or ....
Carbon (............)	.... of hydrocarbons (occurs when there isn't enough .... for ....).	Causes .... problems Reduces .... Makes buildings ....
Sulfur dioxide	From .... in fossil fuels that react during	Acid rain oxides mix with .... to form .... 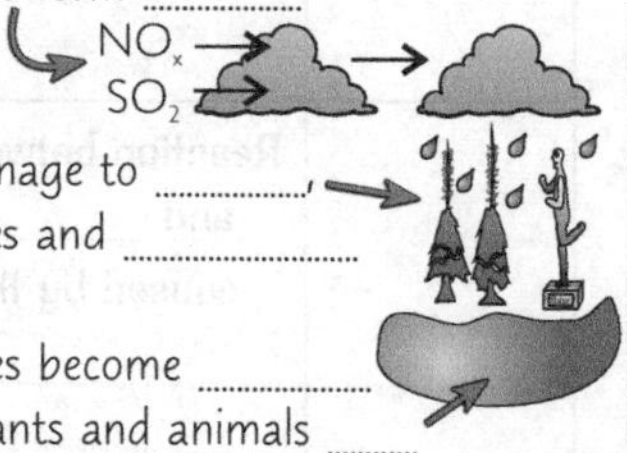 damage to ...., statues and .... lakes become .... — plants and animals ....
Oxides of	Reaction between .... and .... in the air caused by the ...., e.g. in car engines.	

Hydrogen as a Fuel for Vehicles

Advantages	Disadvantages
Very ______ — only waste product is ______.	Need a ______ ______.
Obtained from a ______ resource (______), so ______.	Manufacturing hydrogen is ______, and often uses ______ from fossil fuels.
Can be obtained from the ______ produced by the cell when used in fuel cells.	Hard to ______.

Second Go: ...../...../.....

Pollutants and Fuels

Air Pollution

Fossil fuels contain …… .

This can happen in …… …… .

Pollutant	Formation	Effects
	…… ……  water vapour …… …… …… ……	Stops …… …… around the body — this can cause …… or …… .
	…… …… (occurs when …… ……).	
		…… oxides …… …… 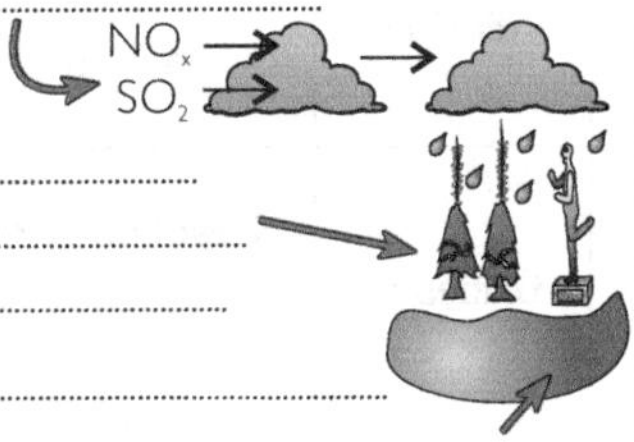 …… …… …… …… ……
	Reaction between …… and …… in the air caused by the …… …… .	

Hydrogen as a Fuel for Vehicles

Advantages	Disadvantages
Can be obtained from	

The Atmosphere

First Go: ..... /..... /.....

Volcanic Gases

Intense ___ ___ released gases.

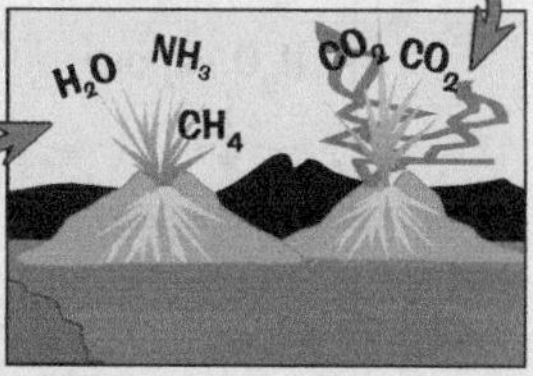

Early atmosphere probably contained mainly ___ with some ___ and small amounts of ___.

The early atmosphere contained virtually no ___.

Absorption of Carbon Dioxide

___ condensed to form oceans.

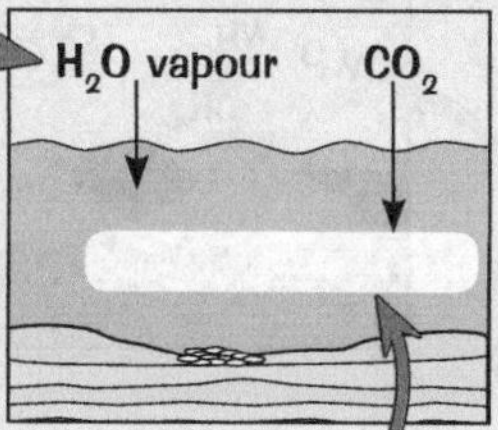

CO_2 gas ___ in the oceans.

This caused an overall ___ in atmospheric CO_2.

Increase in Oxygen

When green ___ evolved, they began to ___.

Photosynthesis:

Removes ___ from the air.

Produces ___.

Over time, ... in the air gradually ...., and .... decreased.

Today's Atmosphere

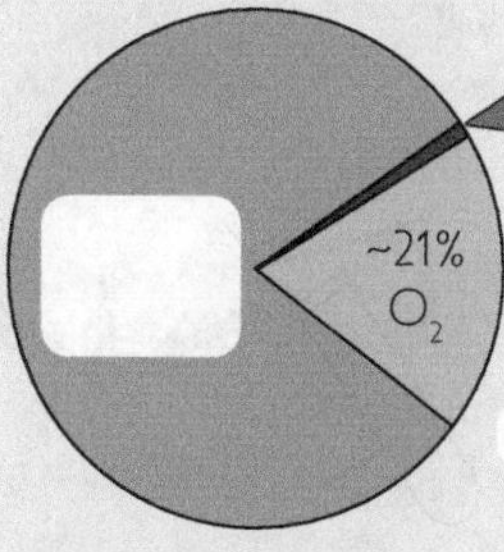

Test for Oxygen Gas

Oxygen will ___ a glowing splint.

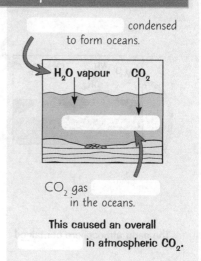

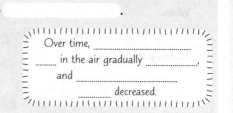

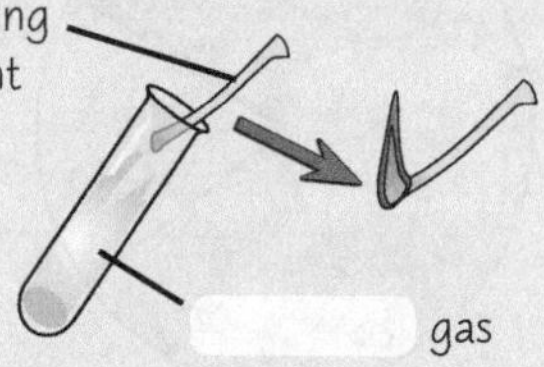

Second Go:
...../...../.....

The Atmosphere

Volcanic Gases

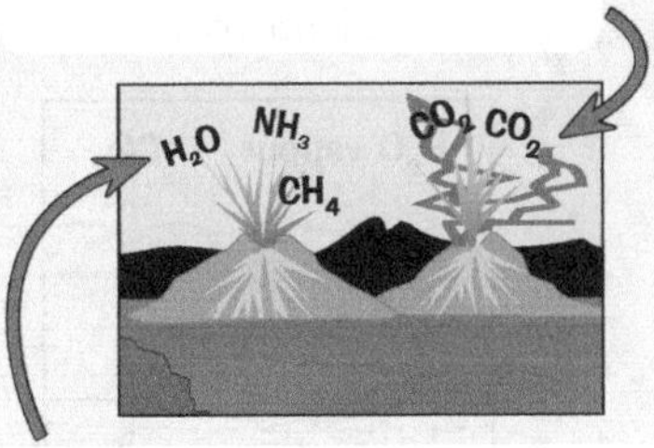

The early atmosphere contained

Absorption of Carbon Dioxide

to form oceans.

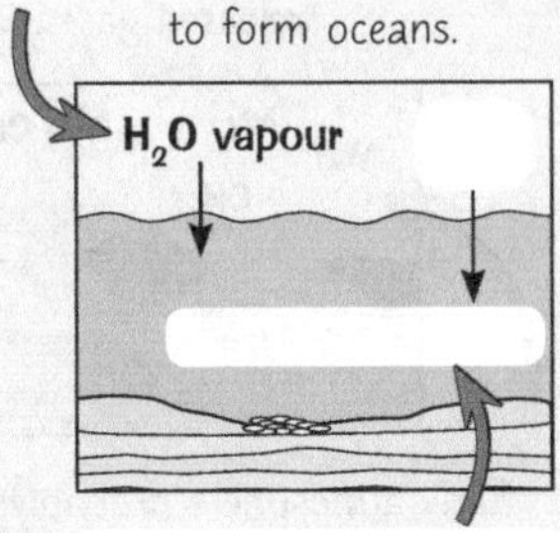

This caused

Increase in Oxygen

When

Photosynthesis:

Over time, ...
....
....
....
....

Today's Atmosphere

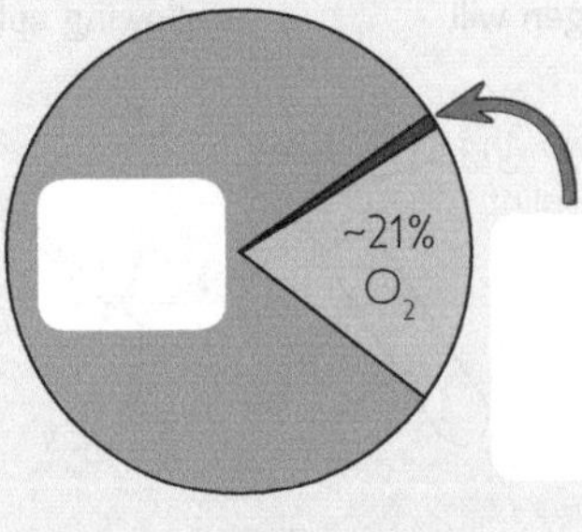

Test for Oxygen Gas

Oxygen will .

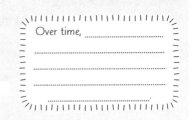

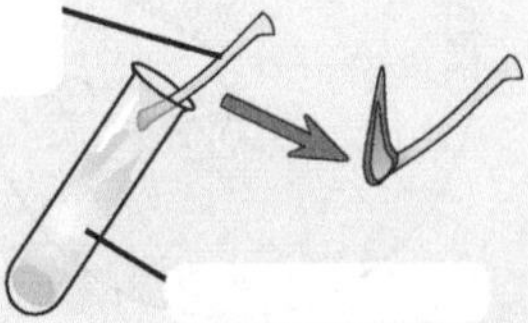

Greenhouse Gases & Climate Change

First Go: ..... /..... /.....

The Greenhouse Effect

Greenhouse Gases		
carbon dioxide		

GREENHOUSE EFFECT — when greenhouse gases in the ______ absorb ______ ______ and re-radiate it in all directions, including back towards Earth, helping to keep the ______ .

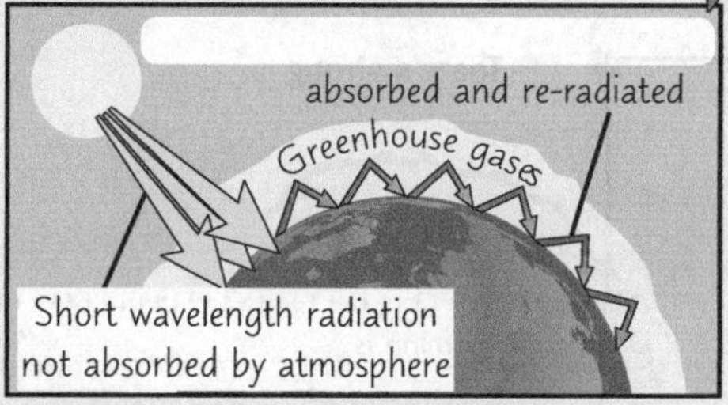

Human Activities

Increased population means more ______, because more:

- Fossil fuels ______ for energy — more ______ released.
- Deforestation — less ______ removed by ______ .
- Farming — more ______ produced.

There's strong correlation between increased levels of .... and ....

.... is a type of climate change that can cause ....

Climate Change Consequences

Two possible consequences of climate change:

1. Flooding due to the ______ ______ causing sea levels to rise.
2. Changing ______ patterns.

Historical Climate Data

- Less ______ and less ______ ______ than modern data.
- Hard to ______ ______ .

Ways of Reducing CO_2 Emissions

Individuals

- .... instead of driving.
- Turn down ....

Governments

- Use legislation and .... incentives.
- Fund .... into ....

Second Go: ..... /..... /.....

Greenhouse Gases & Climate Change

The Greenhouse Effect

Greenhouse Gases		

GREENHOUSE EFFECT — when greenhouse

Human Activities

Increased means more , because more:

Fossil fuels

Deforestation —

Farming —

There's strong

Global warming is ....
....
....

Climate Change Consequences

Two possible consequences of climate change:

1

2 Changing .

Historical Climate Data

Ways of Reducing CO_2 Emissions

Individuals

-
-

Governments

-
-

Mixed Practice Quizzes

There's a lot to learn there, but p.113-118 will help you understand the gases in our atmosphere, as well as helping you to answer these quiz questions.

Quiz 1

Date: ...... / ...... / ......

1) Give one human activity that contributes to increased levels of carbon dioxide in the atmosphere.
2) Give two advantages of using hydrogen as a fuel for vehicles.
3) Roughly what percentage of the atmosphere today is nitrogen?
4) Name a pollutant that can react with water in clouds to form acid rain.
5) Describe a test for oxygen gas.
6) Give one way that an individual can reduce their CO_2 emissions.
7) What caused an increase in oxygen in the early atmosphere?
8) How did the oceans form from the early atmosphere?
9) Which pollutant formed from the incomplete combustion of fossil fuels can lead to fainting, coma or death?
10) How does the greenhouse effect affect the temperature of the Earth?

Total:

Quiz 2

Date: ...... / ...... / ......

1) Give two problems caused by soot.
2) Name three greenhouse gases.
3) How were gases released into the early atmosphere?
4) Name a product of photosynthesis.
5) How is sulfur dioxide produced from fossil fuels?
6) Describe one possible negative effect of climate change.
7) Give two disadvantages of using hydrogen as a fuel for vehicles.
8) Which atmospheric gas is absorbed by green plants for photosynthesis?
9) True or false? The Earth's atmosphere absorbs more long wavelength radiation than short wavelength radiation.
10) Roughly what percentage of Earth's atmosphere today is oxygen?

Total:

Mixed Practice Quizzes

Quiz 3

Date: ...... / ...... / ......

1) Give two ways that governments can help to reduce CO_2 emissions.
2) How do greenhouse gases in the atmosphere keep the Earth warm?
3) True or false? Global warming is a type of climate change.
4) Which gases probably made up Earth's early atmosphere?
5) True or false? When hydrogen is burned as a fuel, the waste products are carbon dioxide and water.
6) Give one problem associated with increased carbon monoxide in the air.
7) Which gas makes up approximately 78% of the atmosphere today?
8) How can burning fuel lead to the production of oxides of nitrogen?
9) How did the formation of oceans lead to a decrease in the amount of carbon dioxide in the atmosphere?
10) Name one element which is often found as an impurity in fossil fuels.

Total:

Quiz 4

Date: ...... / ...... / ......

1) Give one problem caused by sulfur dioxide pollution.
2) Give two problems associated with historical climate data.
3) Which of these is a greenhouse gas — oxygen, nitrogen or methane?
4) Name one gas that makes up a small proportion of Earth's atmosphere today.
5) What happens to a glowing splint if it is placed in a test tube of oxygen?
6) True or false? The Earth's early atmosphere probably contained mainly carbon dioxide.
7) Name two pollutants produced by the incomplete combustion of a fuel.
8) Give one problem caused by acid rain.
9) True or false? Hydrogen is easy to store.
10) Give one human activity that contributes to increased levels of methane in the atmosphere.

Total:

Tests for Ions

First Go: ..... /..... /.....

Chemical Tests

Tests should be ______ — it's not useful if ______ give you the ______ result.

Test for Halides

Add dilute ______ followed by ______ solution to mystery solution.

Chloride (______) ions give a ______ precipitate.

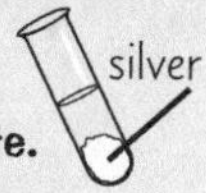
silver chloride

______ (Br^-) ions give a ______ precipitate.

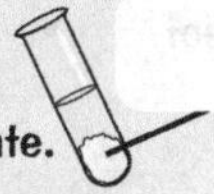

______ ions give a yellow precipitate.

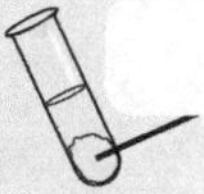

Test for Sulfates

Add ______ hydrochloric acid followed by ______ solution to mystery solution.

If sulfate (______) ions are present, a ______ will form.

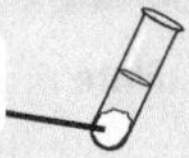

Test for Carbonates

Add a couple of drops of ______.

Mixture will .... if carbonate ions are ....

↓

Connect the ______ to a test tube of ______.

↓

Carbonate ions (______) react to form ______ ______, which will turn the limewater ______.

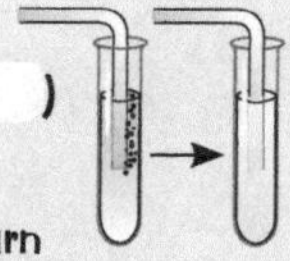

Test for Cations with NaOH

Test for ______ cations:

Add a few drops of ______ (NaOH) solution to mystery solution.

Metal Ion	Colour of Precipitate
Calcium, Ca^{2+}	
	Blue
Iron(II), Fe^{2+}	
Iron(______), ______	Brown
______, Al^{3+}	White

Redissolves in ______ NaOH to form a colourless solution.

Test for ______ ions:

Add ______ solution to mystery solution and gently ______.

If ammonium (______) ions are present, ______ (NH_3) will be given off.

↓

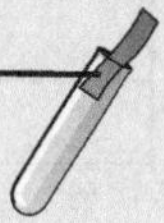
Ammonia gas turns ______ red litmus paper ______.

Second Go: ..... /..... /.....

Tests for Ions

Chemical Tests

Tests should be

Test for Halides

Add dilute

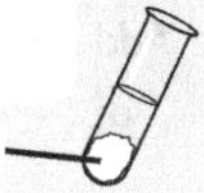

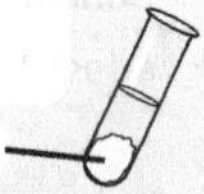

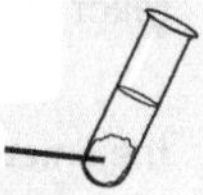

Test for Sulfates

Add dilute

If sulfate

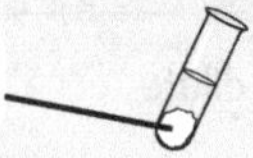

Test for Carbonates

Mixture will ....

Add

Connect

Carbonate ions

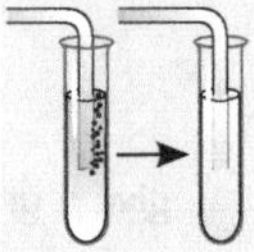

Test for Cations with NaOH

Test for :

Add

to mystery solution.

Metal Ion	Colour of Precipitate
Calcium, Ca^{2+}	
	Blue
Iron(II), Fe^{2+}	
	White

Test for :

Add

If ammonium

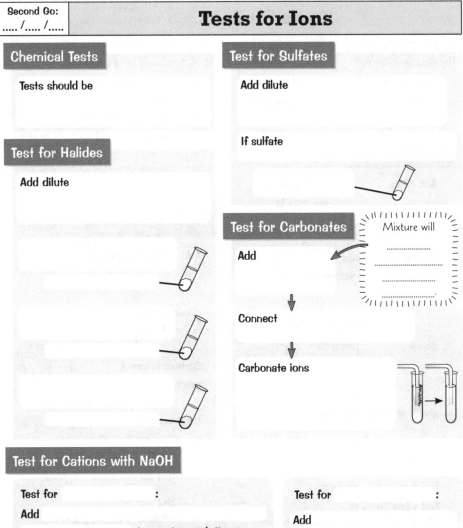

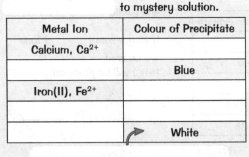

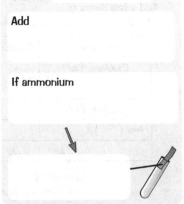

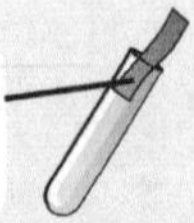

More Tests and Flame Photometry

First Go: ..... /..... /.....

Flame Tests for Metal Cations

Calcium ions	ions	Potassium ions	ions	ions
	Na^+			Cu^{2+}
orange-red flame	flame	flame	red flame	flame

Disadvantage of flame tests — if the sample of metal ions, the flame colours of some ions may be by .

Three Advantages of Instrumental Analysis

INSTRUMENTAL ANALYSIS — that use .

1. Sensitive — can detect
2. Fast — tests can be
3. — don't involve human

Two Uses of Flame Photometry

Flame photometry is an example of

....

1. Identifying ions in — each ion produces a spectrum so you can with .

If .... are present in a sample, the spectrum will be ....

....

2. Determining the of ions — this can be calculated from the of the lines on the .

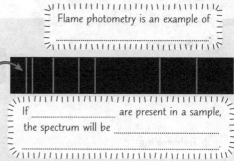

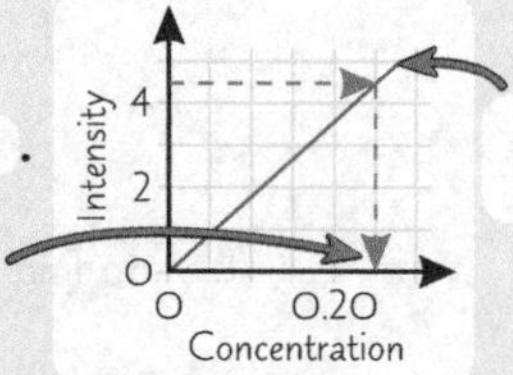

Read from the curve to find that corresponds to .

Second Go: ...../...../.....

More Tests and Flame Photometry

Flame Tests for Metal Cations

Calcium

Sodium

Potassium

Lithium

Copper

Disadvantage of flame tests —

Three Advantages of Instrumental Analysis

INSTRUMENTAL ANALYSIS — .

1. **Sensitive —**
2. — tests can be
3.

Two Uses of Flame Photometry

1. **Identifying**
2. **Determining**

.... is an ....

If .... are present in a sample, the spectrum will be ....

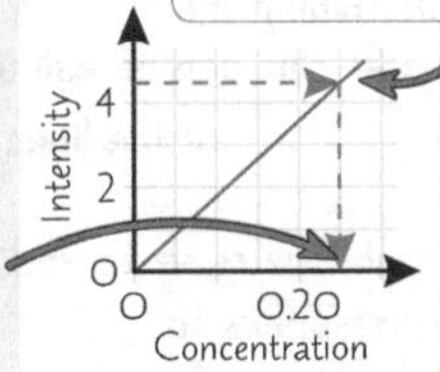

to find .

Types of Hydrocarbons

First Go: ..... /..... /.....

Alkanes

ALKANES — the ______ type of hydrocarbons, containing only ______.

Name	Methane		Propane	
Formula		C_2H_6	C_3H_8	
Structure		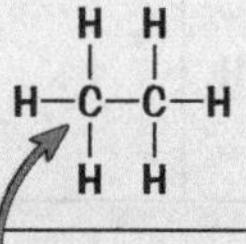		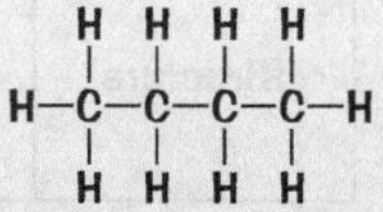

All atoms have formed single covalent bonds with ______ ______ as possible — alkanes are ______.

Alkenes

ALKENES — ______ that have one ______ functional group.

Functional group — a .... in a molecule that .... how that molecule ....

Name		Propene		But-2-ene
Formula	C_2H_4	C_3H_6		
Structure	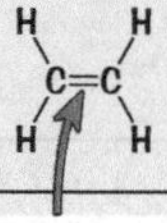		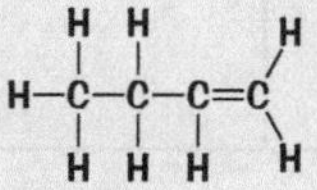	

Alkenes are ______ — double bond can ______ to form other bonds.

Alkenes can undergo ______ where another substance ______ the C=C ______, e.g. ethene reacts with bromine:

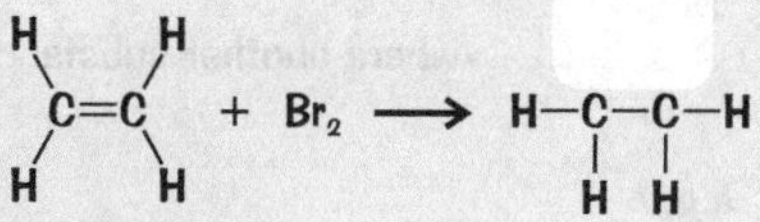

Test for Alkenes

Add alkene to ______

______ ______

Bromine water stays .... if an .... is added.

Combustion

Alkanes and alkenes burn in ______.

Hydrocarbons are ______ during ______:

hydrocarbon + ...

↓

.... + ...

Second Go: ..... /..... /.....

Types of Hydrocarbons

Alkanes

ALKANES —

Name	Methane			
Formula				
Structure		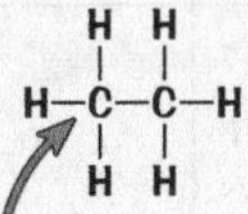		

All atoms have

Alkenes

Functional group — ....
....
....
.... typically ....

ALKENES —

Name		Propene		
Formula				
Structure	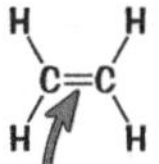			

Alkenes are

Alkenes can

where another substance

,

e.g. :

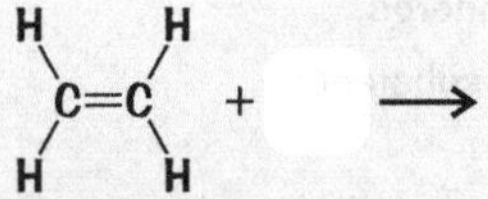

Test for Alkenes

Add

Bromine water
....
....
....

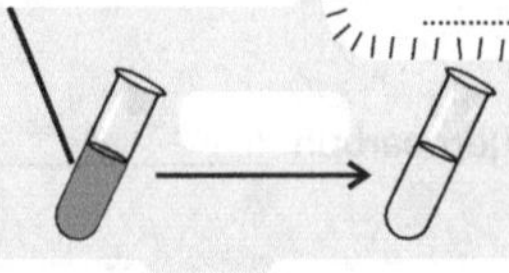

Combustion

Alkanes and alkenes .

Hydrocarbons are

.... + ...

.... + ...

Mixed Practice Quizzes

Hopefully you've brushed up on tests for ions, because it's time for tests for knowledge... Have a go at these quizzes covering p.121-126 — enjoy!

Quiz 1

Date: ...... / ...... / ......

1) Give one use of flame photometry.
2) What would you see if you shake an alkene together with bromine water?
3) What colour is a precipitate of silver bromide?
4) How can you identify ammonia gas?
5) Describe a chemical test you could perform to identify iron(III) ions in solution.
6) Which metal ion burns with a yellow flame?
7) What makes alkanes saturated?
8) How many carbon atoms are present in a molecule of propene?
9) What is a functional group?
10) Why should chemical tests be unique?

Total:

Quiz 2

Date: ...... / ...... / ......

1) How can you test for carbonate ions?
2) Describe how you would test for the presence of sulfate ions in a solution.
3) Give an example of a method of instrumental analysis.
4) What does the line spectrum for a sample containing multiple ions consist of?
5) Which ions form a yellow precipitate with silver nitrate and nitric acid?
6) What is the chemical formula of ethene?
7) What colour precipitate is formed when NaOH is added to a solution containing Cu^{2+} ions?
8) What is the functional group in an alkene?
9) Is the compound with the chemical formula C_3H_8 an alkane or an alkene?
10) Describe two tests you could do to confirm if a solution contains Ca^{2+} ions.

Total:

Mixed Practice Quizzes

Quiz 3

Date: ...... / ...... / ......

1) What is the chemical formula of methane?
2) What is observed when dilute hydrochloric acid and barium chloride solution are added to a solution containing sulfate ions?
3) What is added to a mystery solution to test for the presence of halides?
4) What colour is the flame when you burn potassium ions?
5) Give two advantages of instrumental analysis.
6) What colour is the precipitate formed when NaOH solution is added to a solution containing Fe^{2+} ions?
7) What are alkanes?
8) Does a saturated compound contain any carbon-carbon double bonds?
9) Describe how the C=C bond in an alkene reacts with bromine.
10) Give a disadvantage of using a flame test to identify metal ions.

Total:

Quiz 4

Date: ...... / ...... / ......

1) What are the products of complete combustion of a hydrocarbon?
2) Which metal ion burns with a red flame?
3) Describe how you could test for the presence of NH_4^+ ions in solution.
4) What do you observe when carbon dioxide is bubbled through limewater?
5) What is the positive result of a test for chloride ions in a solution?
6) How many hydrogen atoms are there in a molecule of propane?
7) Describe how you could test for the presence of alkenes in solution.
8) Describe how flame photometry can be used to determine the concentration of ions in solution.
9) Name two alkenes with the chemical formula C_4H_8.
10) Describe a chemical test that you can use to distinguish between a solution containing Al^{3+} ions and a solution containing Ca^{2+} ions.

Total:

Addition Polymers

First Go: ..... /..... /.....

Addition Polymerisation

POLYMERS — substances made by ______ lots of ______. They have a high ______.

ADDITION POLYMERISATION — when molecules with ______ join together in ______.

Monomer

'n' means there can be ______ of monomers.

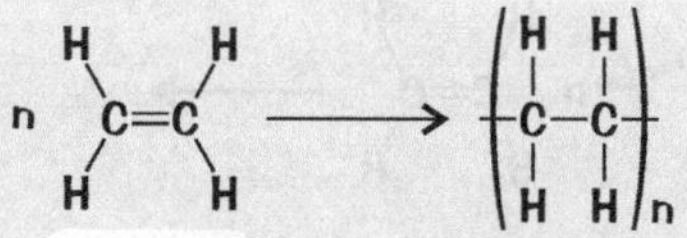

Poly(ethene)

Polymers are named after .... they're formed from.

Other ______ form in the same way — double bonds open up to join ______.

Drawing Polymers

Four steps for drawing ______ of a polymer from its ______:

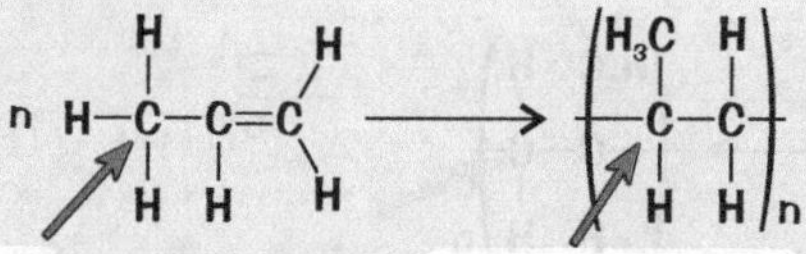

To draw .... from ...., just .... the method below.

1. Draw the ______ and replace the ______ with a ______.
2. Add an extra ______ to each ______.
3. Add ______ in the same way that they ______ the double bond.
4. Add ______ and '   '.

Uses of Polymers

	Properties	Uses
Poly(ethene)	............, cheap, electrical insulator	carrier bags, ...
	flexible, ..., tough, mouldable	............, ropes
.... (PVC)	............, cheap	
Poly(tetrafluoroethene) (............)	unreactive, tough, ...	............, waterproof clothing

Second Go: /..... /.....	# Addition Polymers

Addition Polymerisation

POLYMERS —

ADDITION POLYMERISATION —

'n' means

$$n \quad \begin{array}{c} H \quad H \\ | \quad | \\ C=C \\ | \quad | \\ H \quad H \end{array} \longrightarrow$$

Polymers are
....
....
....
....
....
....

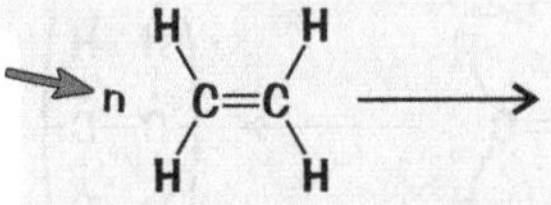

Other addition polymers

Drawing Polymers

Four steps for

$$n \quad \begin{array}{c} H \quad H \quad H \\ | \quad | \quad | \\ H-C-C=C \\ | \quad | \quad | \\ H \quad H \quad H \end{array} \longrightarrow \left(\begin{array}{c} H_3C \quad H \\ | \quad | \\ C-C \\ | \quad | \\ H \quad H \end{array} \right)_n$$

To draw the monomer
....
....
....

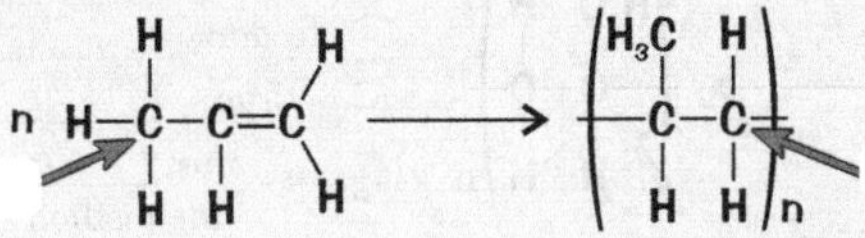

1 Draw

2 Add

3 Add

4 Add

Uses of Polymers

	Properties	Uses
Poly(ethene)		
		plastic crates, ropes
	tough, cheap

More Polymers and Plastics

First Go: ...../...../.....

Condensation Polymers

CONDENSATION POLYMERS — polymers formed from ______ with ______.

In condensation polymerisation, a ______ is ______ for each ______.

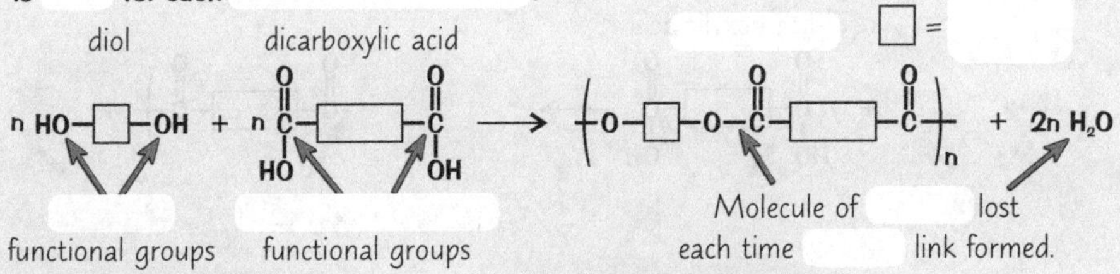

Natural Polymers

DNA — complex molecule that contains ______.

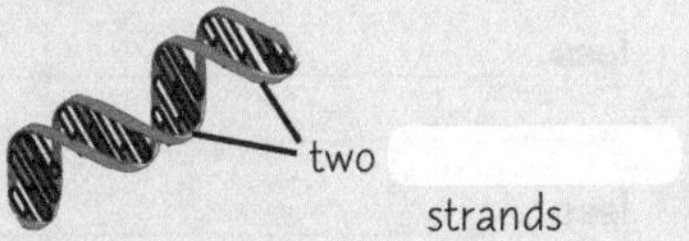

There are .... different ....

STARCH — a ______ made from ______.

Sugars are small molecules containing ______, ______ and ______.

PROTEINS — ______ polymers of ______.

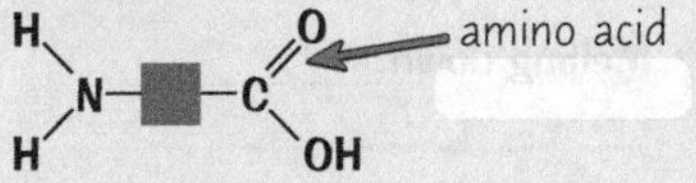

Proteins have many uses in the ...., e.g. in ....

Recycling Plastics

Advantages
• Less plastics have to be .... — this means: less .... waste going to .... less .... and toxic gases released by ....
• Generally uses .... than making new plastics, which are made from .... (finite resource).
• Generally saves .... and creates jobs.

Disadvantages
• Must be .... before melting down — .... and ....
• Melting down can still release ....
• Over time, strength of polymer .... — can't recycle same polymer ....

Second Go: ..... /..... /.....

More Polymers and Plastics

Condensation Polymers

CONDENSATION POLYMERS —

In condensation polymerisation,

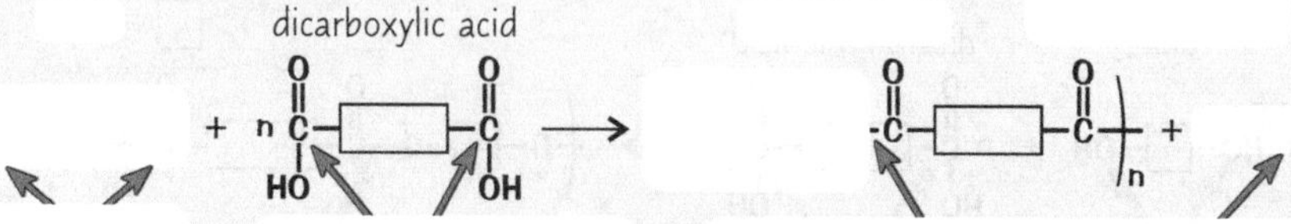

Natural Polymers

DNA —

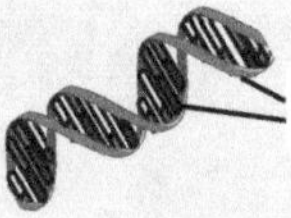

There are ....
....

STARCH —

Sugars are

PROTEINS —

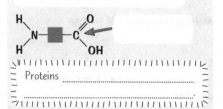

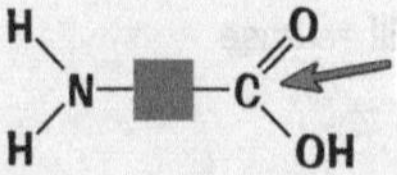

Proteins ....
....

Recycling Plastics

Advantages	• Less .... — this means: less .... less .... • Generally uses fewer ...., which are made ....…. • Generally ....
Disadvantages	• Must be .... • Melting down .... • Over time, ... of polymer .... — can't recycle ....

Alcohols and Carboxylic Acids

First Go: ..... /..... /.....

Alcohols

ALCOHOLS — a compound containing .

Name	Methanol	Ethanol		
Formula				C_4H_9OH
Structure	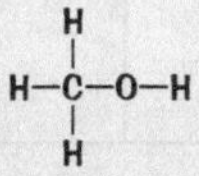		e.g. 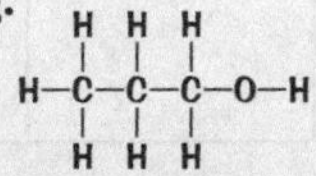	e.g.

Make from alcohols by heating alcohol with . ← This is a reaction as a molecule of is lost from the alcohol.

Carboxylic Acids

CARBOXYLIC ACIDS — a compound containing a functional group.

Carboxylic acid solutions have the same properties as solutions.

Name		Ethanoic acid	Propanoic acid	
Formula	HCOOH		C_2H_5COOH	
Structure		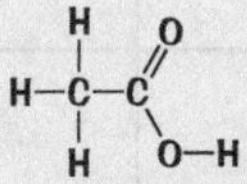		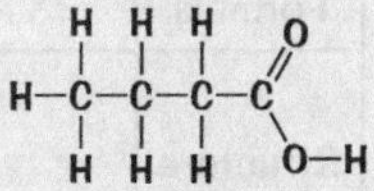

Carboxylic acids can be made by alcohols — e.g. can be oxidised to form ethanoic acid.

Members of a .... have similar reactions as .... they share a ....

Fermentation

FERMENTATION — process where a converts solutions of (e.g. sugar) into .

sugar → +

Optimum conditions for	
°C	conditions

Fermentation only produces a of ethanol — yeast when concentration too .

Fractional distillation is used to the ethanol solution:

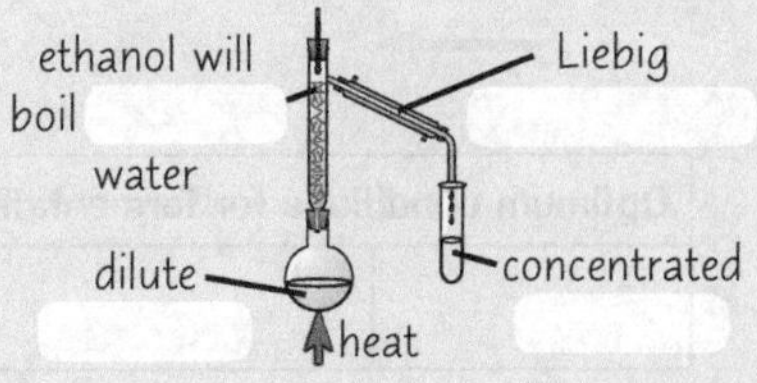

Second Go: ..... /..... /.....

Alcohols and Carboxylic Acids

Alcohols

ALCOHOLS — a compound .

Name				
Formula				
Structure			**e.g.**	**e.g.**

Make

This is a

Carboxylic Acids

CARBOXYLIC ACIDS —

Carboxylic acid solutions

Name				
Formula				
Structure				

Carboxylic acids can

Members of a ....
....
....
....

Fermentation

FERMENTATION —

$\rightarrow$ +

Optimum conditions for fermentation	

Fermentation only

Fractional distillation **the ethanol solution:**

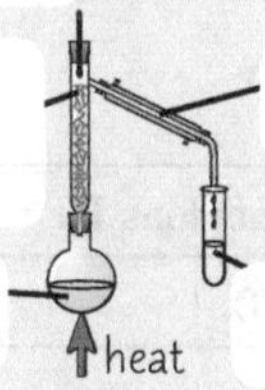

Nanoparticles and Materials

First Go: ..... /..... /.....

Particle Sizes

	Diameter (..........)
.... and simple	0.1 – 1
Nanoparticles	

contain a few [ ] atoms

surface area to volume ratio = [ ]

Nanoparticles have a high [ ] ratio compared to [ ] — this gives them different [ ] to [ ].

Uses of Nanoparticles

- [ ] — more surface area means [ ] rate of reaction.
- [ ] — small particles could be absorbed right into [ ] cells.
- Cosmetics, e.g. [ ] — small particles provide more [ ] and don't leave [ ] on skin.

There is a risk that nanoparticle products could have .... on health. E.g. nanoparticles could .... in cells over time if they don't get ....

Materials and their Uses

You can use .... about properties of materials to assess their .... for different uses.

		Properties	Uses
	POLYMERS Many small .... bonded in long	• Thermal and .... insulators • Often ...., can be .... • Lower .... than metals, ceramics	• .... casing • Carrier bags, ...
CERAMICS	.... Soft mineral hardened by	• Can be .... • .... • Brittle • Glass is	• Bricks • ....
CERAMICS	.... E.g. soda-lime glass made by heating ...., ... and		•
	.... One material (.........................) embedded in another (.........................).	Depend on materials used. • E.g. concrete is strong and .... • .... is strong and	• .... • Sports cars
		• Thermal and electrical .... •	• Wiring

Second Go:
..... /..... /.....

Nanoparticles and Materials

Particle Sizes

	Diameter (.........)
.... and simple	

contain

=

Nanoparticles have

Uses of Nanoparticles

-
-
-

There is a risk that nanoparticle products .... E.g. nanoparticles could .... if they ....

Materials and their Uses

You can use .... of materials to assess their ....

		Properties	Uses
	POLYMERS	• • •	• • Carrier bags, ...
CERAMICS		•	• •
CERAMICS		• • •	•
	.... One material	Depend on .... • •	• •
		• •	•

Mixed Practice Quizzes

Wow, that was a whole lot of facts. If polymers and materials aren't your thing yet, don't worry — here are some quizzes on p.129-136 to see where you're at.

Quiz 1

Date: ...... / ...... / ......

1) What is the functional group of an alcohol?
2) Give two disadvantages of recycling plastics.
3) What is lost each time a new bond forms in condensation polymerisation?
4) What method can be used to concentrate a dilute solution of ethanol?
5) True or false? Nanoparticles have a small surface area to volume ratio.
6) What does 'n' mean in the formula for a polymer?
7) Name three addition polymers.
8) How many functional groups are present on each monomer in condensation polymerisation?
9) What type of compound is butanoic acid?
10) What properties of carbon fibre make it a good material for sports cars?

Total:

Quiz 2

Date: ...... / ...... / ......

1) Name the polymer produced from ethene monomers.
2) Give one problem associated with disposing of plastics by burning them.
3) What is fermentation?
4) Give three properties of ceramics.
5) What monomers join together to form a protein?
6) What feature must molecules have in order to join together to produce an addition polymer?
7) How many different nucleotide monomers are there in DNA?
8) Are carboxylic acids strong or weak acids?
9) Give two examples of common uses of nanoparticles.
10) What is produced when an alcohol is dehydrated?

Total:

Mixed Practice Quizzes

Quiz 3

Date: ...... / ...... / ......

1) Give two types of ceramics.
2) What is the typical diameter of a nanoparticle?
3) Are proteins produced by condensation or addition polymerisation?
4) What is a polymer?
5) State two uses of PTFE.
6) Give the chemical formula for propanol.
7) What is the functional group for carboxylic acids?
8) Give two benefits of reducing the amount of plastic that must be disposed of.
9) What name is given to the small molecules which join together to form a polymer?
10) Give the word equation for the reaction involving sugar and a yeast enzyme.

Total:

Quiz 4

Date: ...... / ...... / ......

1) What type of polymerisation also produces small molecules such as water?
2) Name one naturally occurring polymer made from sugar monomers.
3) Give an example of a risk posed by the use of nanoparticles.
4) What are composites?
5) Which properties of poly(ethene) make it suitable for use in electrical wire insulation?
6) Describe how to draw the displayed formula of a polymer when you know the structure of the monomer.
7) What are the optimum conditions for fermentation?
8) True or false? Members of the same homologous series undergo similar chemical reactions.
9) Give three advantages of recycling plastics.
10) Give one way that carboxylic acids can be formed from another compound.

Total:

Core Practicals 1

First Go: ..... /..... /.....

Two Techniques for Investigating Composition of Inks

1. ______ can separate solvent from dyes if solvent ______:

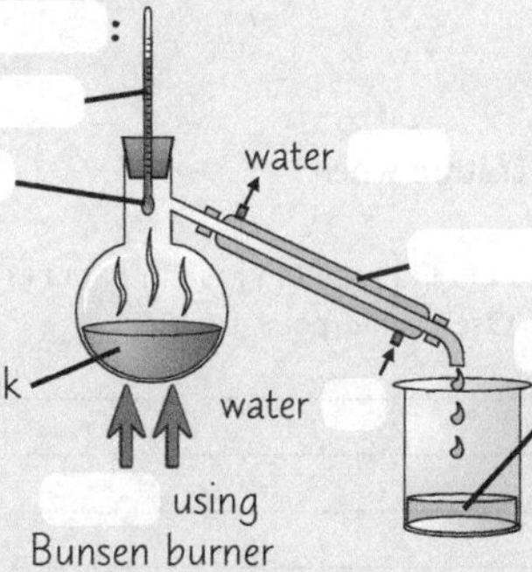

Use boiling point to help .... — e.g. if boiling point is ...., the solvent is quite likely ....

2. ______ can separate out different dyes:

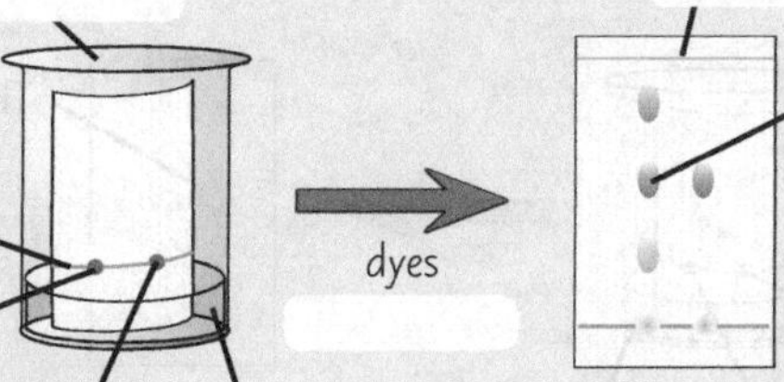

The experiment should ______ to see if the spots still match in ______.

Dyes can be identified by ______ ______ to known compounds.

Four Steps to Investigate Neutralisation

1. Add ______ of calcium oxide to ______ of dilute hydrochloric acid.

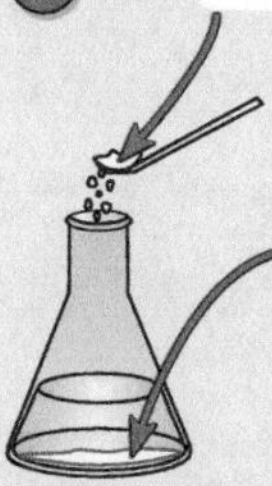

2. Record ______ after reaction finishes using ______ or ______.
3. Keep adding ______ ______ and measuring ______ until some calcium oxide remains at the bottom — this means ______.
4. Plot a graph to show how ______ changes with ______:

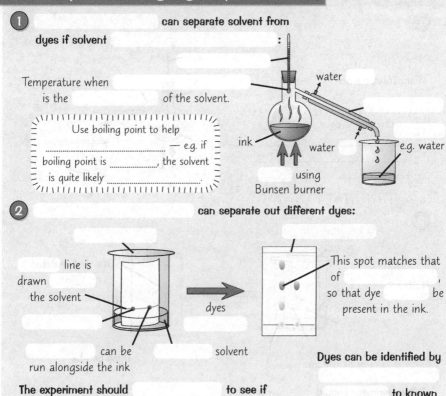

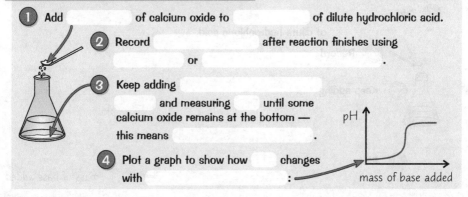

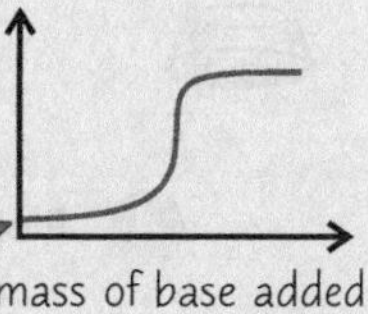

Second Go: ...../...../.....

Core Practicals 1

Two Techniques for Investigating Composition of Inks

1

Temperature when

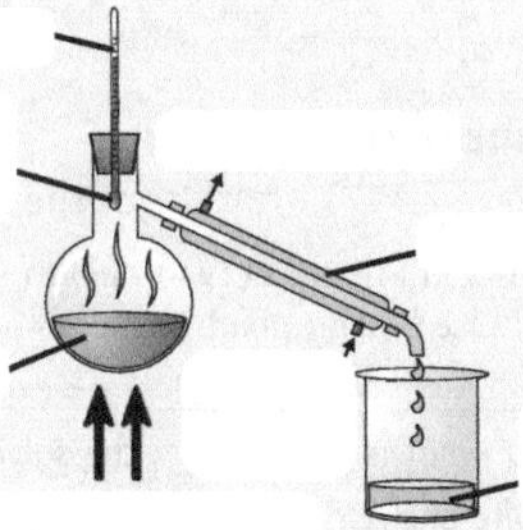

Use boiling point to ....
....
....
....
....

2

is drawn

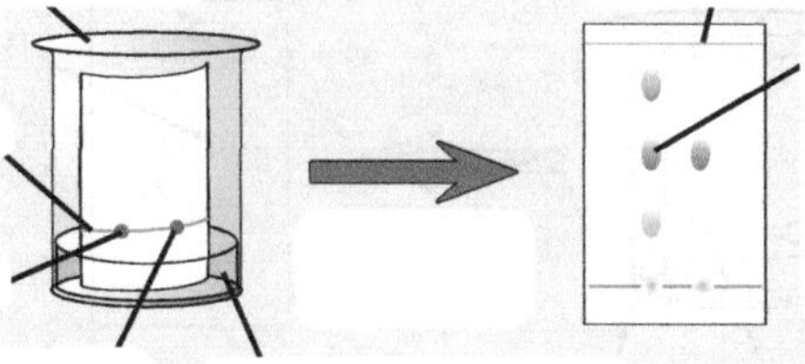

This spot matches

alongside the ink

Dyes can be

The experiment should

Four Steps to Investigate Neutralisation

1 Add

of dilute hydrochloric acid.

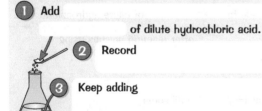

2 Record

3 Keep adding

pH

4 Plot

mass of base added

Core Practicals 2

First Go: ...../...../.....

Making Copper Sulfate

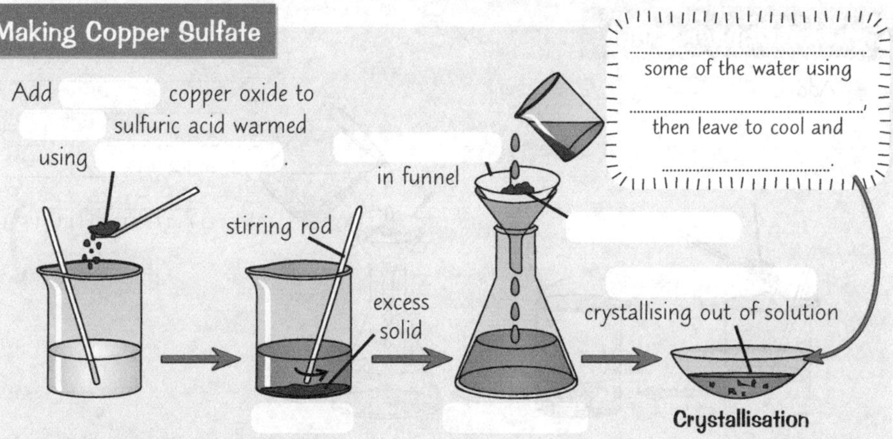

After crystallising the soluble salt, .

Electrolysis of Copper Sulfate Solution

Using inert (graphite) electrodes:

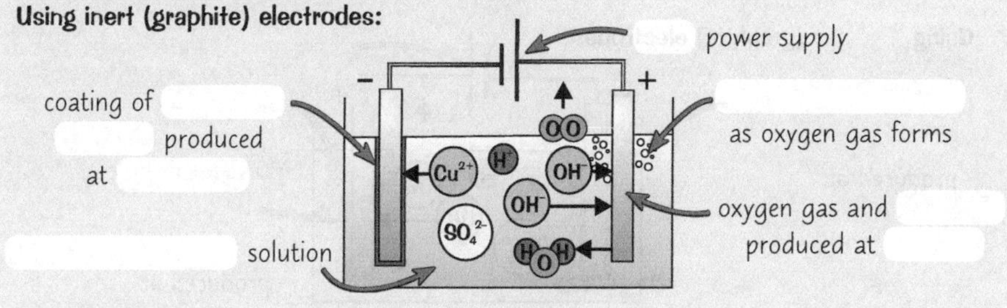

Using copper electrodes:

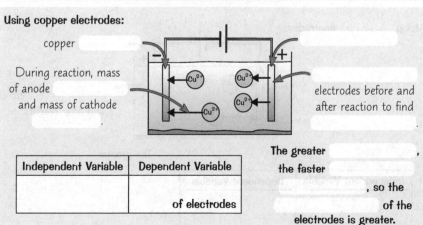

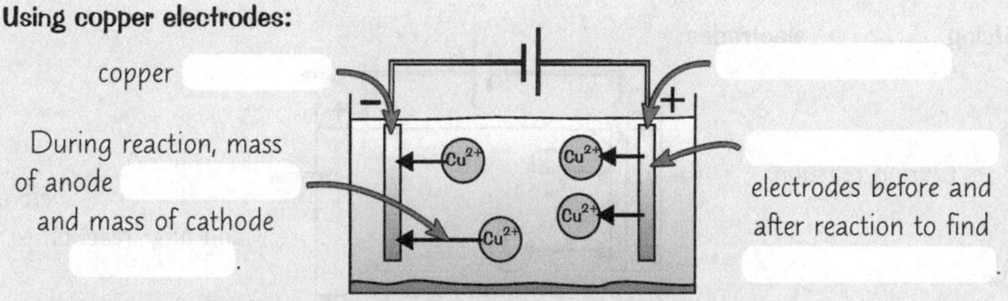

Independent Variable	Dependent Variable
	of electrodes

The greater , **the faster** , **so the** **of the electrodes is greater.**

Second Go: ..... /..... /.....	Core Practicals 2

Making Copper Sulfate

Add

....
....
....
....,
then leave to ....
....

After the soluble salt, .

Electrolysis of Copper Sulfate Solution

Using (graphite) electrodes:

produced at

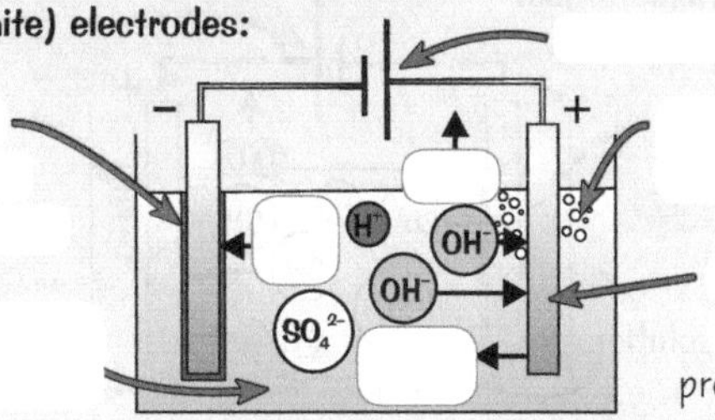

produced at

Using electrodes:

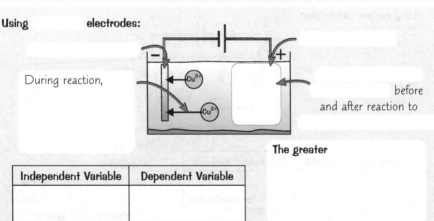

During reaction,

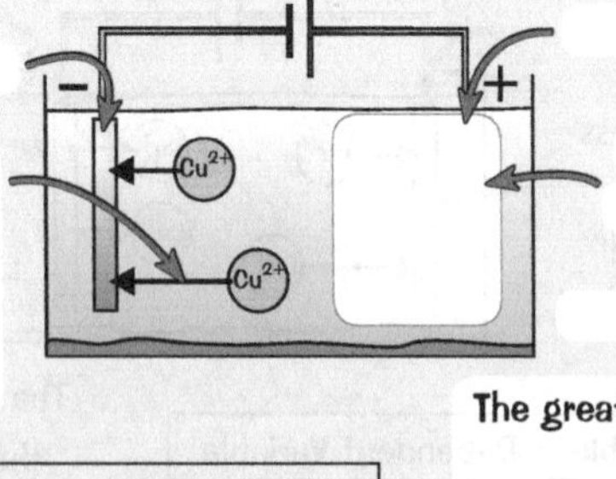

before and after reaction to .

The greater

Independent Variable	Dependent Variable

Core Practicals 3

First Go: ..... / ..... / .....

Titrations

Do a .... first to find the approximate end point.

.... containing a strong acid of ....

Use a .... to add the acid to the ....

Take an .... from the ....

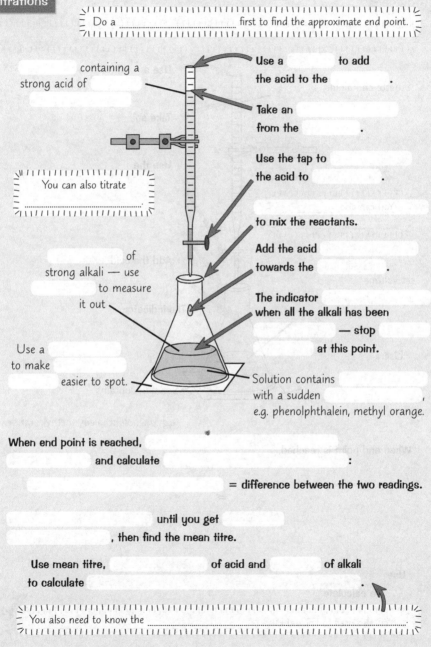

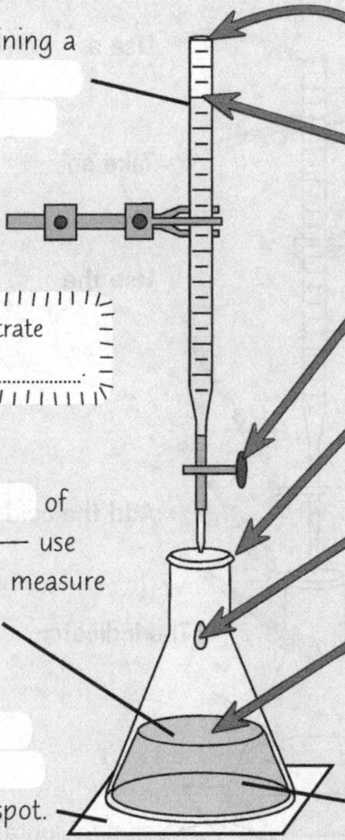

You can also titrate ....

Use the tap to .... the acid to ....

.... to mix the reactants.

.... of strong alkali — use .... to measure it out

Add the acid .... towards the ....

The indicator .... when all the alkali has been .... — stop .... at this point.

Use a .... to make .... easier to spot.

Solution contains .... with a sudden ...., e.g. phenolphthalein, methyl orange.

When end point is reached, ... and calculate ....:

.... = difference between the two readings.

.... until you get ...., then find the mean titre.

Use mean titre, ... of acid and .... of alkali to calculate ....

You also need to know the ....

Second Go: ...../...../.....

Core Practicals 3

Titrations

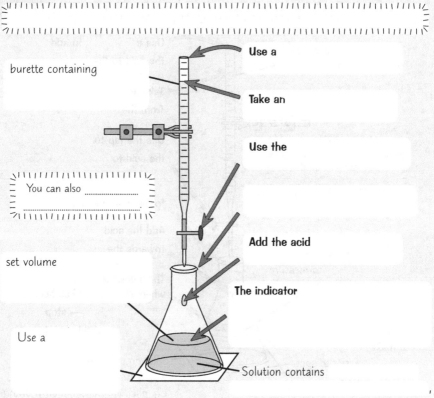

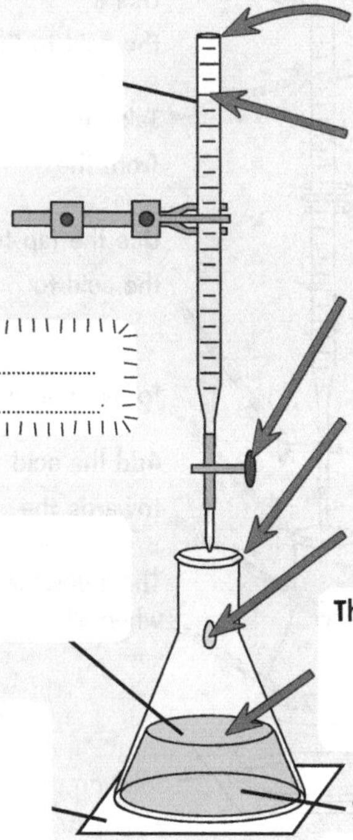

burette containing

Use a

Take an

Use the

You can also ....

....

Add the acid

set volume

The indicator

Use a

Solution contains

,

e.g. phenolphthalein, methyl orange.

When end point is reached,

=

Use

to calculate

You also need to know the ....

Core Practicals 4

First Go: ..... /..... /.....

Two Ways of Measuring Rates of Reaction

1 The given off

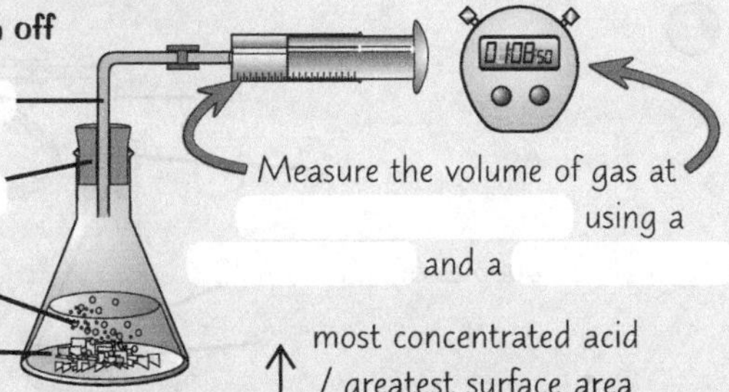

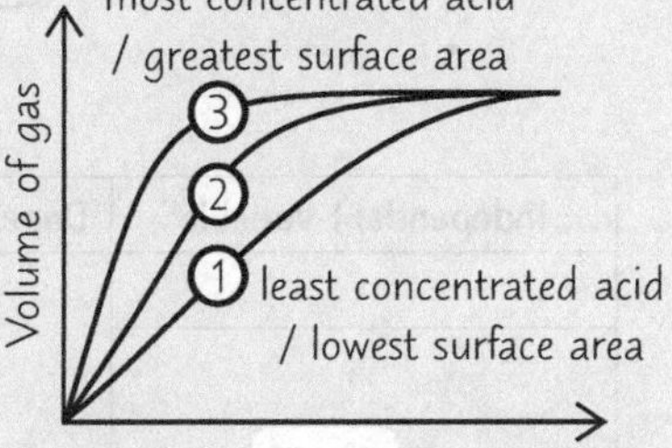

Independent Variable	Dependent Variable
of acid or of marble chips	released

When rate of reaction is given off in a time interval.

2

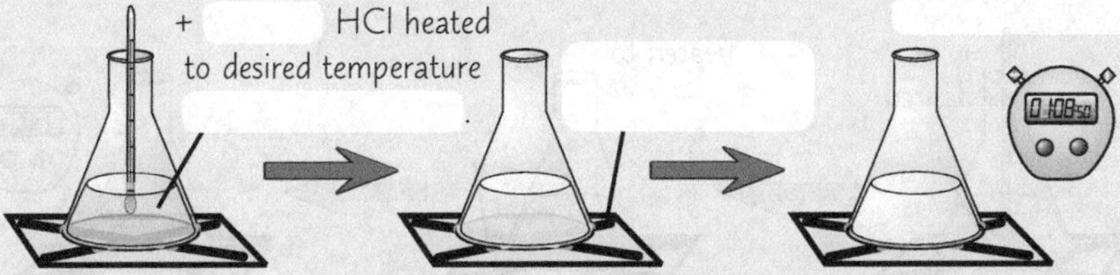

The results of this experiment are ....

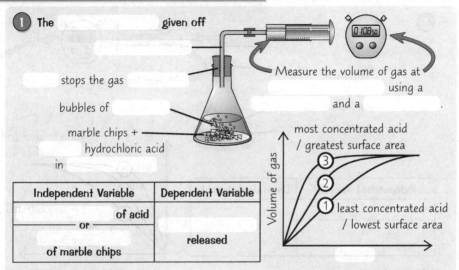

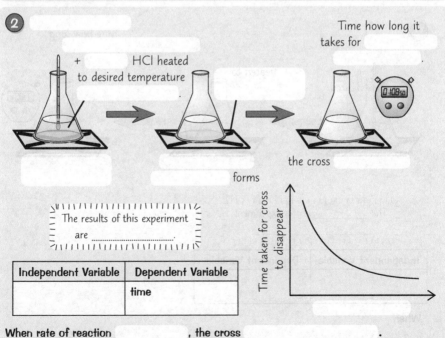

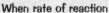

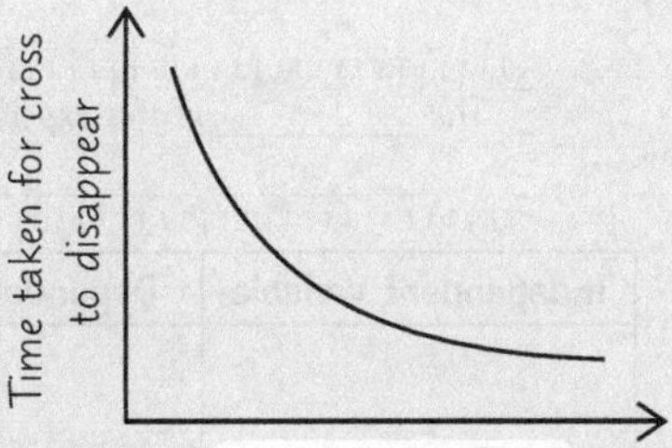

Independent Variable	Dependent Variable
	time

When rate of reaction , the cross .

Second Go: ..... /..... /.....

Core Practicals 4

Two Ways of Measuring Rates of Reaction

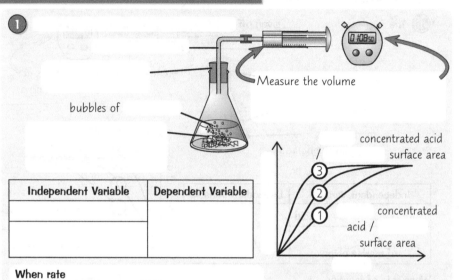

1

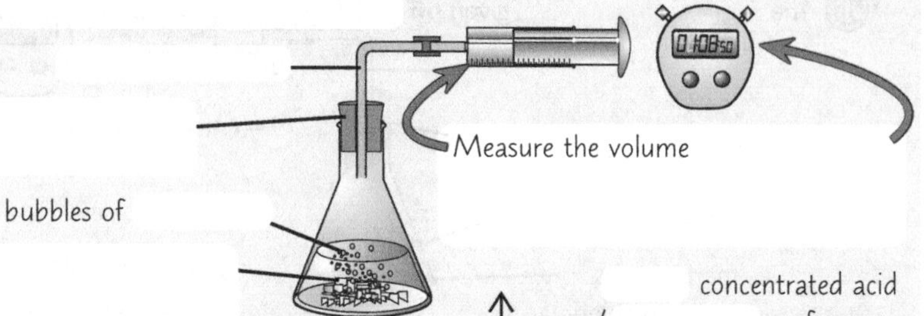

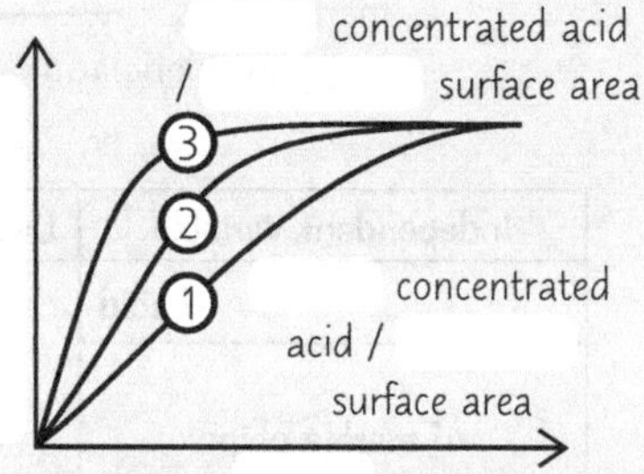

Independent Variable	Dependent Variable

When rate

2

The .... of this experiment ....

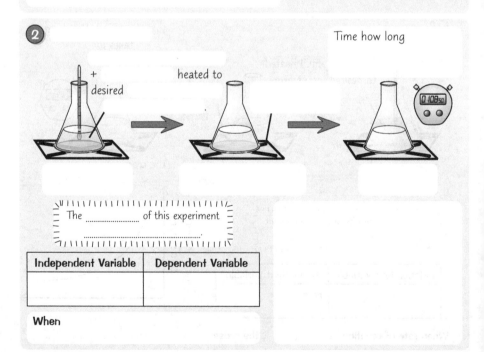

Independent Variable	Dependent Variable

When

Core Practicals 5

First Go: ..... /..... /.....

Identifying Ions

Ion	Test	Observation
Cl^-	Add dilute , then silver nitrate solution.	precipitate
		precipitate
		yellow precipitate
SO_4^{2-}	Add dilute , then solution.	
CO_3^{2-}	Add test tube to a test tube of limewater.	limewater
NH_4^+	Warm with . with damp red litmus paper.	litmus paper

Some metal ions form a

with NaOH solution.

Ca^{2+}	white
Cu^{2+}	
	green
Fe^{3+}	

Precipitate in excess NaOH to form a .

Three steps for performing flame tests

1. Clean a loop — dip it in then rinse with .
2. into the sample.
3. Hold the loop in a flame.

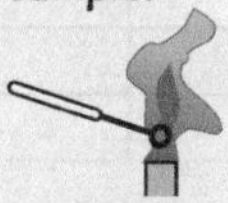

Li^+	Na^+			
red		lilac	orange-red	

Combustion of Alcohols

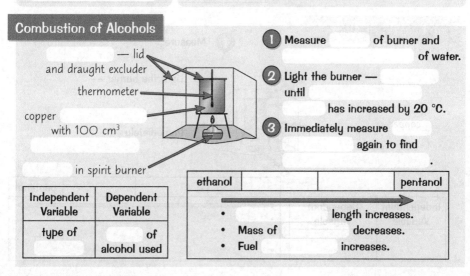

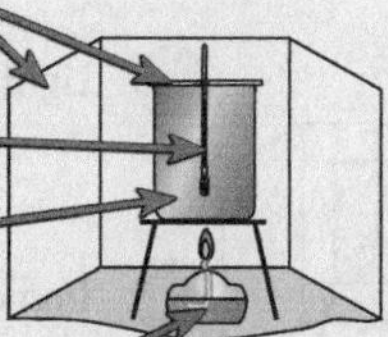

1. Measure of burner and of water.
2. Light the burner — until has increased by 20 °C.
3. Immediately measure again to find .

Independent Variable	Dependent Variable
type of	of alcohol used

ethanol			pentanol

- length increases.
- Mass of decreases.
- Fuel increases.

Second Go: ..... /..... /.....

Core Practicals 5

Identifying Ions

Ion	Test	Observation
	Add dilute	
	Add dilute	white precipitate
CO_3^{2-}	Add dilute	
	litmus paper.	

Add

Some metal ions

Ca^{2+}	
Fe^{3+}	

Precipitate

Three steps for

1. Clean a
2.
3. Hold the loop

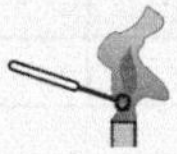

	Na^+			
		lilac	orange-red	

Combustion of Alcohols

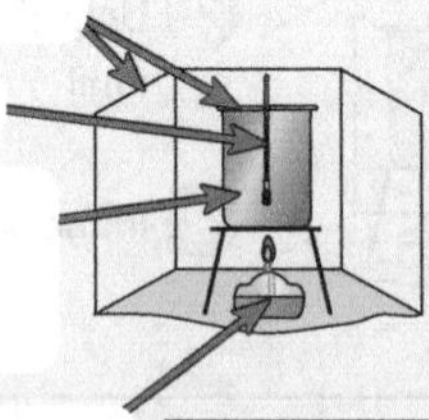

copper

1. Measure
2. Light the burner —
3. Immediately

Independent Variable	Dependent Variable

			pentanol

→

-
-
-

Mixed Practice Quizzes

Feeling practical after p.139-148? Don't worry — you won't have to build any flat-pack furniture or anything like that. Just see how you get on with these quizzes.

Quiz 1

Date: ...... / ...... / ......

1) Describe how to use distillation to separate a solvent from dyes in an ink.
2) True or false? When making copper sulfate crystals, the excess copper oxide is removed by evaporation.
3) Give one limitation of measuring the rate of a reaction by observing a colour change in the reaction mixture.
4) Which metal ion burns with a blue-green flame?
5) How should you fill the burette with acid when preparing a titration?
6) What is the dependent variable in the experiment where copper sulfate solution is electrolysed using copper electrodes at different currents?
7) Describe the shape of a graph showing how pH changes as excess base is gradually added to a solution of acid.
8) In chromatography, where should the pencil line be relative to the solvent?
9) Describe how to crystallise a soluble salt out of a filtered solution.
10) True or false? Alcohols with longer carbon chains are more efficient fuels.

Total:

Quiz 2

Date: ...... / ...... / ......

1) Give two possible dependent variables for measuring the rate of a reaction.
2) Suggest an acid and a base that can be used to investigate neutralisation.
3) What reactants could you use to make copper sulfate crystals?
4) How can you measure the boiling point of a solvent using simple distillation?
5) What type of power supply is used for electrolysis?
6) What should you use to measure out the set volume of solution in a titration?
7) Give a possible independent variable when investigating the rate of a reaction.
8) How can you find the mass of alcohol used to heat a volume of water?
9) Give the positive result of a test for I^- ions using silver nitrate and nitric acid.
10) In electrolysis, how is the change in mass of a copper electrode found?

Total:

Mixed Practice Quizzes

Quiz 3 Date: / /

1) Give two ways you could measure the pH when investigating neutralisation. ☐

2) Describe what to do before dipping a loop into a sample for a flame test. ☐

3) True or false? The solvent used in an ink can be separated from the dyes using simple distillation if it has the lowest boiling point. ☐

4) What forms when using inert electrodes to electrolyse copper sulfate solution? ☐

5) Which ion forms a white precipitate with hydrochloric acid and barium chloride? ☐

6) Describe how to calculate the volume of acid added from a burette. ☐

7) Give a reason why it is useful to repeat a paper chromatography experiment. ☐

8) How can you measure the volume of gas produced in a reaction? ☐

9) How can you make copper sulfate crystals from copper oxide and sulfuric acid? ☐

10) What is the dependent variable in the experiment where different alcohols are used as fuels to heat a set volume of water by a set amount? ☐

Total: ☐

Quiz 4 Date: / /

1) Describe how you could insulate a copper calorimeter. ☐

2) How does carbon chain length affect the mass of fuel needed to heat water? ☐

3) When producing copper sulfate crystals, which reactant should be in excess? ☐

4) Describe how to investigate how pH changes during a neutralisation reaction. ☐

5) How could you confirm the identity of a certain dye in a mixture if its spot matches the spot from a pure dye in a chromatogram? ☐

6) When should you stop adding the solution from the burette during a titration? ☐

7) Describe the graph showing time taken for a cross to disappear against temperature for the reaction of hydrochloric acid with sodium thiosulfate. ☐

8) When performing chemical tests, what should you use to add a few drops of reagent to the solution of unknown ions? ☐

9) Describe how to investigate the effect of current on the rate of electrolysis. ☐

10) True or false? When carrying out a titration, the solution with an unknown concentration should be in the burette. ☐

Total: ☐

Apparatus and Techniques

First Go: ..... /..... /.....

Measuring Mass

Transferring solid to ______:

When making a solution, ______ remaining solid out of the ______ with the ______.

or

Find the ______ of the container and ______ before and after you ______.

Three Ways to Measure Liquids

1 Pipette

2 Burette

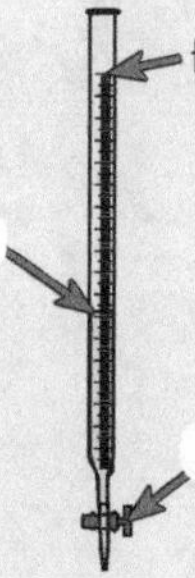

3 Measuring ______

Pick a ______ for volume required.

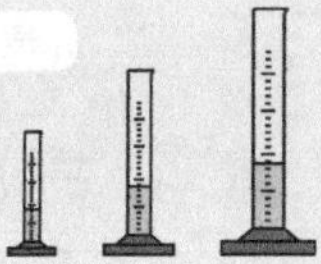

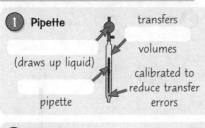

When measuring ______:

Always read the volume from the ______ of the ______.

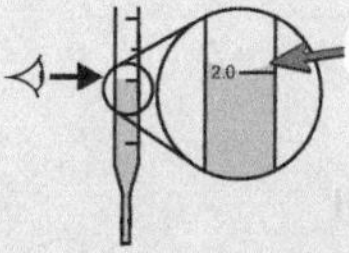

Measuring Time

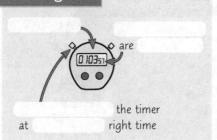

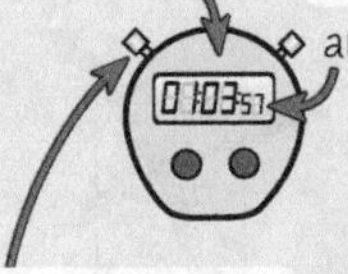

Measuring Temperature

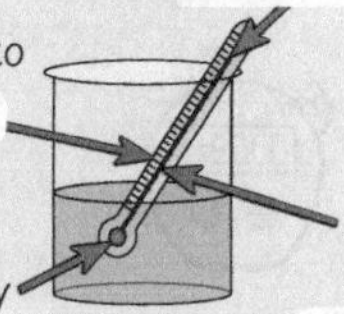

Second Go: ..... / ..... / .....

Apparatus and Techniques

Measuring Mass

solid to :

When making a solution,

or

Find the difference

Three Ways to Measure Liquids

1 Pipette

transfers

calibrated to

2 Burette

scale measures

Volume of liquid used

tap releases

3

Pick a

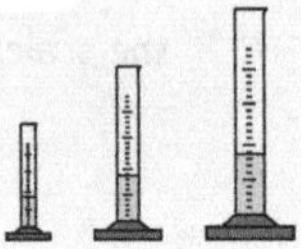

When :

Always read

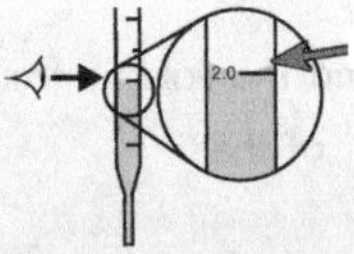

Measuring Time

Measuring Temperature

wait for

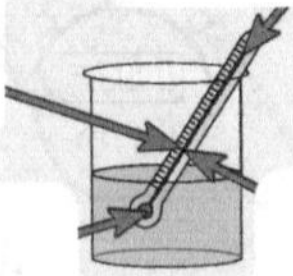

bulb

Practical Techniques

First Go: ..... /..... /.....

Measuring pH

red green purple

indicator:

ACID pH 7 BASE

Litmus:

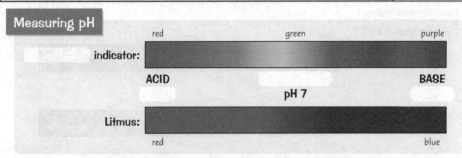

red blue

Indicator solution	Indicator paper
Changes colour of	For testing of solution
Good for showing the in titrations	Use to test gases

pH probes and give a value for pH.

Safety Precautions

to do with your method any experiment.

Use a fume cupboard to avoid .... like chlorine.

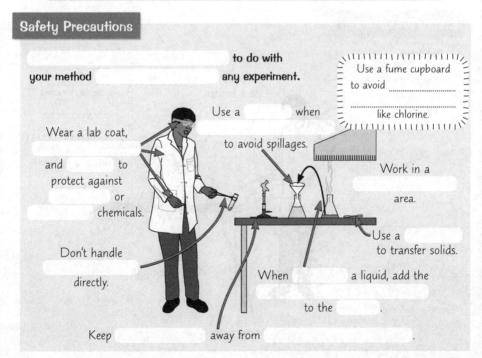

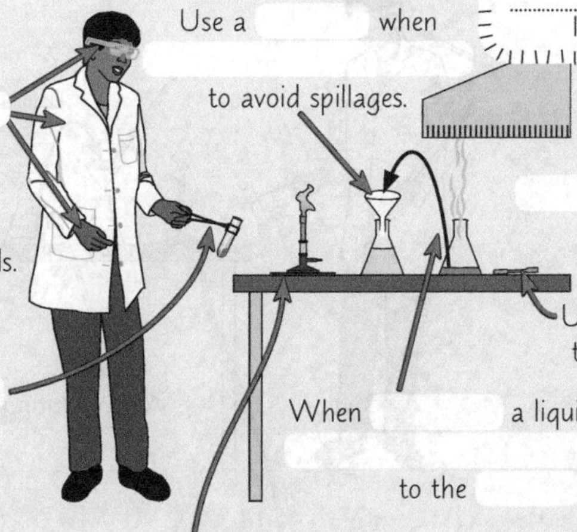

Wear a lab coat, and to protect against or chemicals.

Use a when to avoid spillages.

Work in a area.

Use a to transfer solids.

Don't handle directly.

When a liquid, add the to the .

Keep away from .

Second Go: ..... /..... /.....

Practical Techniques

Measuring pH

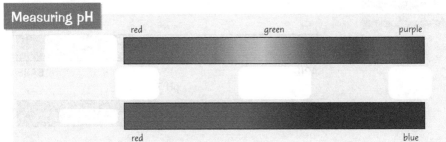

Indicator solution	
Changes	For testing
Good for	Use

pH probes and

Safety Precautions

Read the

Use a funnel

.... to avoid releasing ....

Wear a

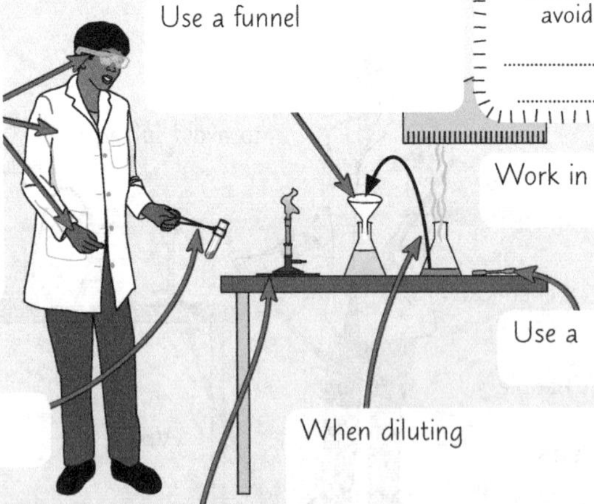

Work in a

Use a

Don't handle

When diluting

away from .

Equipment and Heating Substances

First Go: ..... /..... /.....

Collecting Gases

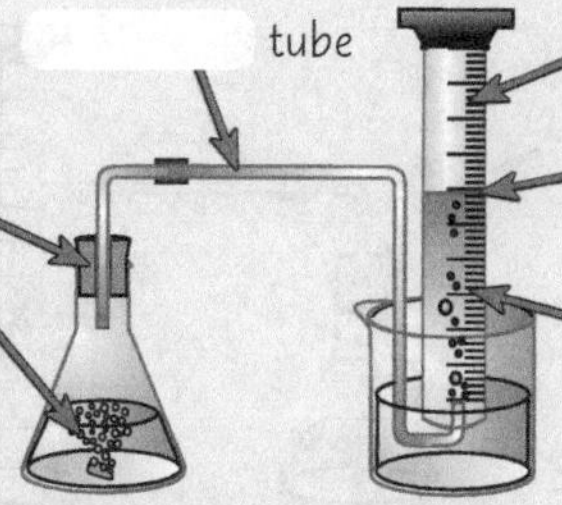

Using a gas syringe is .... than this — some gases .... which affects the amount in the ....

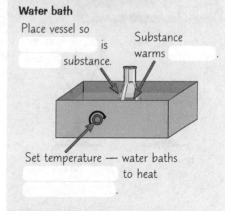

Amount of gas collected is

between the volumes

in the .

Using Bunsen Burners

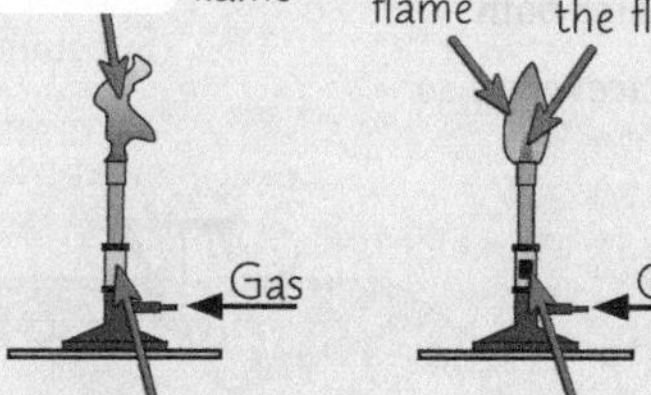

You can use

to show

how apparatus is :

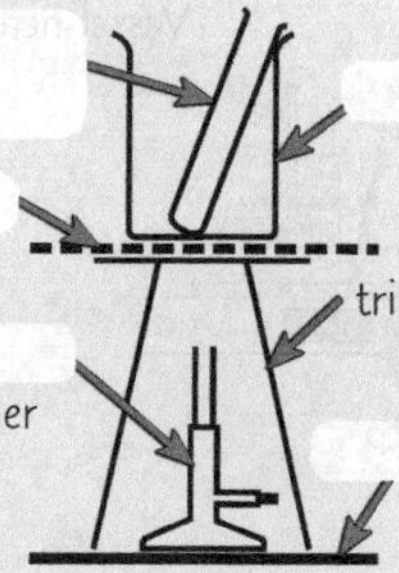

Other Heating Methods

Water bath

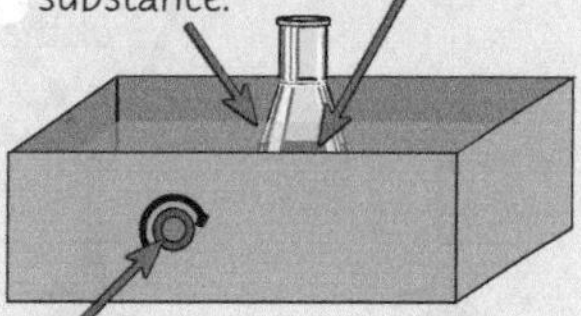

Electric heater

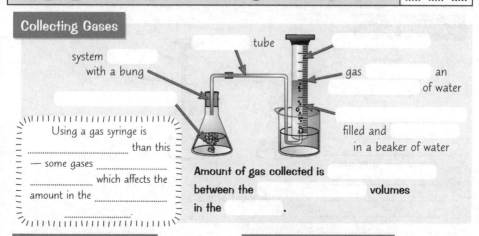

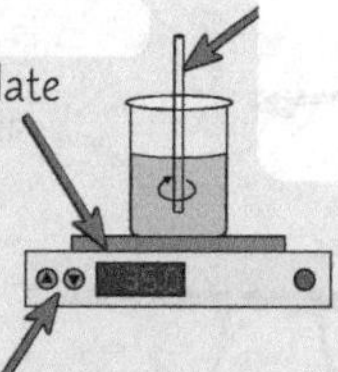

Equipment and Heating Substances

Collecting Gases

system

gas

measuring cylinder

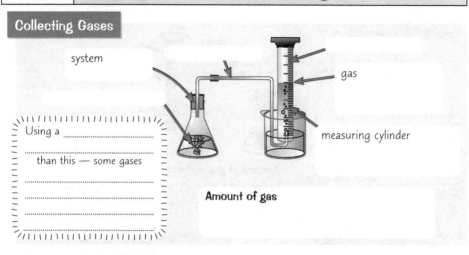

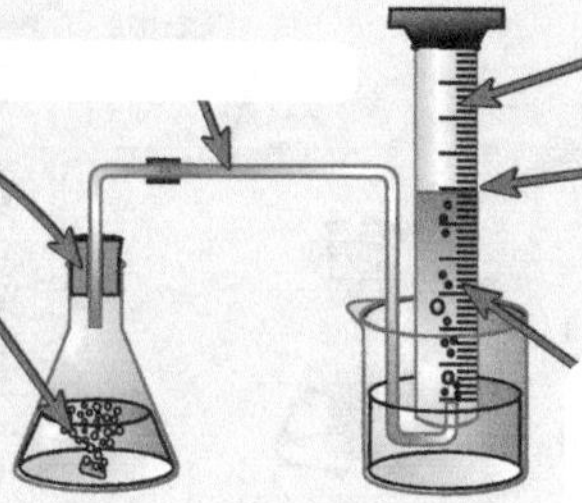

Using a
....
than this — some gases
....
....
....

Amount of gas

Using Bunsen Burners

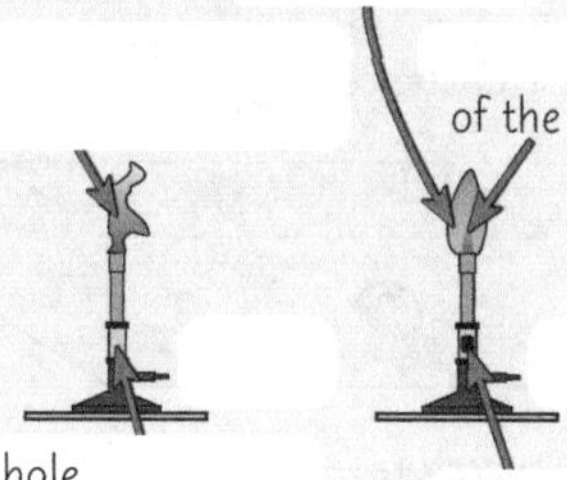

of the

hole

hole

You can use

test
tube

beaker

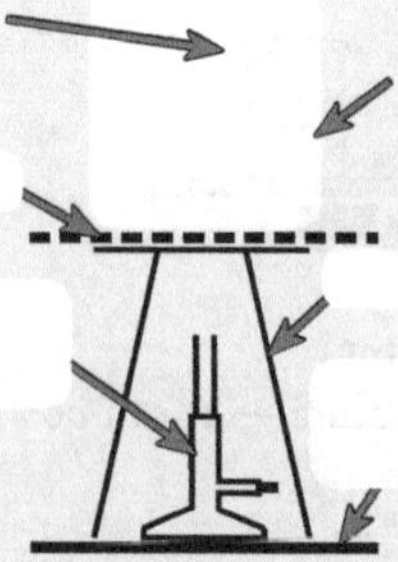

Other Heating Methods

Water bath

Place vessel so

Substance

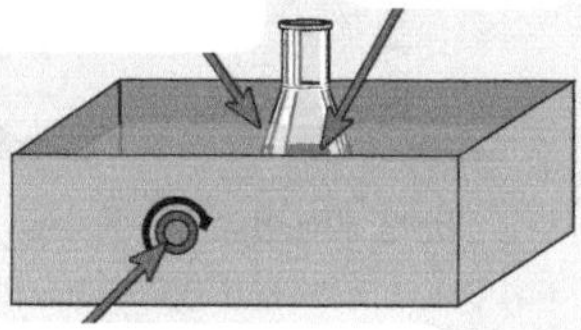

Set temperature —

Electric heater

Vessel heats

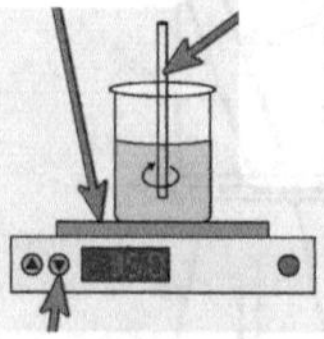

Set to

 ☑ ☑ 😃 ☑

Mixed Practice Quizzes

The final quiz pages of the book... Hooray! Before you start celebrating, use them to check you know all of the practical skills covered on p.151-156.

Quiz 1

Date: ...... / ...... / ......

1) Give two examples of when you'd use indicator paper.
2) How is liquid released from a burette into a container?
3) Give one way you can ensure you are working safely with hot glassware.
4) Describe how to use a measuring cylinder to collect gaseous products.
5) Outline how to measure the mass of a substance using a mass balance.
6) Give one piece of equipment you could use to transfer solid chemicals safely.
7) How can you ensure that a sample is heated evenly by an electric heater?
8) Give an example of when a scientific drawing may be used.
9) True or false? You should measure the temperature of a solution immediately after placing a thermometer in it.
10) Why might using a gas syringe to measure the volume of gas be more accurate than an upturned measuring cylinder?

Total:

Quiz 2

Date: ...... / ...... / ......

1) Describe how to read the volume of a liquid from a scale.
2) What piece of apparatus could you use to measure temperature?
3) Give an advantage of using a pH probe and meter over universal indicator.
4) What is the hottest part of a Bunsen burner flame?
5) Give two ways of heating a sample without using a flame.
6) Give an advantage of using a pipette to transfer a specific volume of liquid.
7) Give a safety precaution you should follow when using flammable chemicals.
8) What is the neutral pH value?
9) Give two methods of collecting the volume of gas produced in a reaction.
10) Give three protective items that should be worn when carrying out an experiment.

Total:

Mixed Practice Quizzes

Quiz 3

Date: ...... / ...... / ......

1) Give an example of when you might use an indicator solution.
2) Describe how a Bunsen burner should look when it is alight but not heating.
3) Give two ways of accurately transferring a mass of solid to a reaction vessel.
4) How do you work out the volume of liquid added from a burette?
5) True or false? Water baths and electric heaters both warm substances evenly.
6) How can you avoid releasing harmful gases from a reaction into the room?
7) Describe how to accurately measure the temperature of a solution.
8) What piece of apparatus can transfer a specific, accurate volume of liquid?
9) What can be used to help seal the system when the gaseous products of a reaction are collected in a filled, upturned measuring cylinder?
10) Compare the heating capabilities of water baths and electric heaters.

Total:

Quiz 4

Date: ...... / ...... / ......

1) What piece of equipment could you use to measure time?
2) True or false? Damp indicator paper can be used to test gases.
3) How could you make sure that all of a solid substance from a weighing container is transferred to a reaction vessel when making a solution?
4) True or false? To safely dilute a liquid, you should add the water to the concentrated substance.
5) How should you place a vessel in a water bath so that its contents are heated evenly?
6) What must be considered when picking a suitably sized measuring cylinder?
7) How should the hole on a Bunsen burner be set when it is used for heating?
8) Give three ways to measure the pH of a solution.
9) How does bubbling gas into a measuring cylinder that has been filled and upturned in a beaker of water allow you to measure its volume?
10) Give one example of when and why you might use a funnel in an experiment.

Total: